Sensational Salads to Cool the Earth

Tastes like Love

Sensational Salads to Cool the Earth

BETH LOVE
with foreword by Neal Barnard, MD

WHOLENESSWORKS
Santa Cruz, California

SENSATIONAL SALADS TO COOL THE EARTH
Copyright 2016 by Beth Love

127 National Street
Santa Cruz, CA 95060
www.wholenessworks.com

Book and cover design by Cathy Krizik.

Author photograph by Russell Downing of russelldowningphotography.com.

All other photographs by Beth Love.

Photo editing by Earl Dotter.

Editing by Alix Schwartz, Beth Freewomon, and Evelyn Avanti.

Printed on paper certified by The Forest Stewardship Council™ (FSC®), The Sustainable Forestry Initiative® (SFI®), and Programme for the Endorsement of Forest Certification™ (PEFC™).

ISBN # 978-0-692-81413-0

Dedication

This book was created for the children of the world and their children after them. May they be healthy and compassionate, and may they live in peace on a planet that abundantly and sustainably supports and nourishes them.

A portion of the proceeds goes to Physicians Committee for Responsible Medicine to support their lifesaving work in research, advocacy, education, systems change, and empowerment.

Acknowledgments

The book you are holding in your hands or reading on your device is truly a labor of love. Though it was birthed through me, it would not have been possible were it not for a tremendously supportive and loving community of book midwives. I have deep and abiding gratitude for each and every person who supported this baby to move through the stages of preconception, gestation, development, and birth. It is quite an honor to have so many people excited about this book, encouraging me, cheering me on, eagerly anticipating the arrival, and celebrating its glorious entry into the world!

I want to start by thanking the Beloved Creator of all things that is always with me, that has given me a life in which to make meaning in a profoundly beautiful creation that is worthy of great stewardship.

I also want to thank my husband, Golden Love, who reminds me of my capacities during my momentary lapses. Golden, your energy, love, encouragement, and support are as present in this book as are my recipes, my photos, my words. Thank you!

I am indebted to the team of professionals who helped transform my text and photos into the beautiful form you see. Co-creating with you has been an absolute delight! Thank you, Alix Schwartz, for being the most phenomenal big sister anyone could every hope for, and for using your considerable editorial talents to make the non-recipe portions of the book stronger, more cogent, and more accessible. Given your high standards, getting your stamp of approval helped me to really see myself as an author. Thank you to my sister in the Spirit, Beth Free-womon, for pouring through the recipes with your big heart, your eagle eye, your expertise in food preparation, and your powerful commitment to consistency. Thank you, fellow vegan activist Evelyn Avanti, for going through the entire book after it was laid out with a powerful eye for detail and a potent spirit of excellence. Thank you, Cathy Krizik, for showering this project with your astounding design capacities, your abundant creativity, and your gracious patience. You caught a glimpse of my vision and brought it gloriously to life.

I needed and received so much support with this project. That support came in various forms, including financial backing. I want to thank every donor who gave to one or both of my fundraising campaigns. Thank you Aden Neumeister, Alix Schwartz, Allison Rhea, Andria M. Wood, Antonina Hines, Barbara Monett, Berenice Amaya-Gonzalez, Beth Freewomon, Betsy Wason, Beverly Boyd, Brenda Shinault, Carrie Burr, Catherine Byrne, Coleen Douglas, Dawni Pappas, Deb Berard, Deb Gillespie, Debbie O'Connor, Debie Nervina, Deborah Stern, Dela Soumitte, Eileen Attanasio, Ellis McCauley, Erica Springer, Fawn Blasey Lustig, Fern Selzer, Francesca Graziano, Francisca & Priya Friday-Pabros, Golden Love, Gretchen Giambra, Jean Rutherford, Jean Sibley, Jennifer Goldbeck, Joan Teitler, Karen Johnson, Karen Menehan, Kate Robinson, Kelly Menehan, Margo Zanzinger, Meghan Green, Michelle Montoya, Muna AlSheikh, Orsolya Salzberg, Paula Lotz, Rachel Dotter, Rainbow Schwartz, Ruth Poe, Scott Palmer, Stan and Fifi Schwartz, Susan Lantis, Taica Patience, Valerie Hayes, Valerie Joi Fiddmont, and Vicki Wynne. Your generous donations of funds inspired me deeply, because I know the full value of what you gave went so far beyond money. Through your donations you invested faith, encouragement, and presence in this project, and I feel sincerely honored.

It has taken support to see myself as a phenomenal chef, and hundreds of eaters over the years have been essential to that transformation. Though I cannot name them all, I want to start by acknowledging the wonderful patrons of the Families Ministry monthly lunch, an event I organized for several years while I was on staff at Inner Light Ministries, and for which I was generally the head chef. Your encouragement, your profuse praise for the food, and your consistent requests for a cookbook were strong motivators in the process of conceiving this book. So many of you told me that you could be vegan if you had regular access to the delicious food you ate at the monthly lunches. I hope this book will help you eat more plants. Thank you so much for moving this project forward with your energy and your prayers!

I also want to acknowledge my home community here at The Love House. I appreciate you all as tasting supporters, and also for your patience with apparently endless kitchen chaos as these recipes were created, tested, and refined over time. Thank you Golden Love, Michael Peck, and Andrew Porter for being the supportive home team during the actual creation of the recipes in this book and the book itself. Thank you Eva Clark and Harley Eblen for being on the home team in the early phases of gestation. Thank you all for taking on the serious responsibility of eating the copious rivers of food that continuously poured through The Love House kitchen!

I also want to thank all of my family members and friends who have encouraged my culinary activities over my whole life. The acknowledgments would go on forever if I named every one of you! In addition to those acknowledged elsewhere, I want to specifically recognize my daughter Eden Love Schwartz, son Adam Blasey, stepdaughter Leisyka Parrott, and father Stan Schwartz for years of encouragement and support. You are all awesome!

There was a special team of testers who took one or more of the recipes after I created them and tried them out in your own kitchens. I learned so much from your feedback and also appreciate your support with posting and tagging on social media. Thank you Alexandra Montreal, Beverly Boyd, Evelyn Avanti, Joselito Laudencia, Judy Jugan, Julie Wooden, Orsolya Salzberg, Quadira, Ruth Poe, and Susan Robinson. Whether or not I took a specific suggestion you made, please know that your collective feedback greatly advanced my understanding of how to codify recipes in ways that could be replicated with fidelity by others. (And thank you for catching omissions!)

When I left my position of almost 20 years as a minister with Inner Light Ministries, I knew there was something else for me to do in the world, but I wasn't clear what that was. Many people attended a series of visionings I hosted to support the birth of a new "something," and that "something" ended up to be a new business, including the Tastes Like Love division and this book series. Thank you for helping me to gain clarity about my current personal mission: to inspire practical and profound choices that promote wholeness and sustainability for individuals, families, communities, the earth, and all her inhabitants. This book is an expression of that calling. Thank you Golden Love, Beverly Boyd, Ruth Poe, Beth Freewomon, Vanessa Wilson, Dawni Pappas, Debbie Bratby, Kimberly Kiefer, Jean Sibley, Eden Love Schwartz, Kate Gilligan, Deb Gillespie, ReGina Chavez, Matthew Marichiba, Serina Marichiba, Maiana Marichiba, Esther Frances, and Kelly and Karen Menehan. Even though the visionings happened months ago, the pictures you drew and the words you spoke call me up and lead the way forward on a daily basis, and I thank you for that.

I also want to acknowledge all of the incredible participants of my culinary classes. You really helped me refine my capacity to translate my apparently innate capacities with food into language that could be understood by others. You also enlarged my audience of tasters and showered me with encouragement, appreciation, and love. Your spirit is in this book series, and I am grateful.

Betsy Wason, how grateful I am for that first conversation we had when I worked up the courage to call you after thinking about it for several months! You were so welcoming and encouraging, so receptive to my offer of partnership with

Physicians Committee for Responsible Medicine. Committing to this partnership helped me stretch beyond my comfort zone because of the strength of my love for the organization and its extraordinary work. Thank you to you and all of the staff of PCRM for your tremendous contributions to human health and nutrition, human-relevant testing and training, and compassion for animals, and thank you for partnering with me to bring this book series out in the world.

A few more specific acknowledgments are in order. Tyler Oxford, thank you for your expert and loving work in capturing my passion so beautifully in the video you made to help with my fundraising campaign and beyond. Russell Downing, you know how to take a picture! Posing for pictures is nowhere near the top of my list of favorite things to do. I appreciate your patience and love in bringing out the best in me for the author photo on the back cover. Chef Ellie Lavender, thank you for your encouragement to see myself as a chef, and your big, generous welcome into the chef community. I also want to acknowledge you, Chef Ellie, and Cierra Savatgy-King for helping me with my steep social media learning curve. You both are making it possible to extend the reach of this work beyond my immediate community. Thank you! Michael Peck, with your big heart and your spirit of service, thank you for keeping my technological environment in order. What a difference it has made in my workflow to have your support, expertise, and tangible contributions!

I also want to acknowledge Kenny and Lauren Gottlieb, the original owners of the tasteslikelove.com domain. Thank you so much for your willingness to support this project with the precious gift of the domain! I so appreciate how you grokked my vision and decided to come on board, and I will always be grateful for your generosity.

This community of midwives is as responsible for the birthing of this book as am I. Readers, you may have a sense of the size and power of this community from these acknowledgments, yet I know there are more supporters I did not name. While it may be impossible to acknowledge each person by name, if you recognize yourself as part of the community that rallied around this creation, please know that I am profoundly moved by your generosity, your love, your encouragement, and your support!

Contents

Foreword

BY NEAL BARNARD, MD

Foods give us wonderful power. They help us stay healthy, help us to be kinder to the animals with whom we share this planet, and, as you'll see in the pages of this book, allow us to protect the planet itself.

If you are opening this book to find creative new foods for your table, you'll find an abundance of them. And you'll find much more. Even though the focus is on delicious and healthful salads and dressings, Beth Love shares her vision for cooling this Earth we live on and a strategy that really works.

A plant-based diet is a treat for your body. It helps you maintain a healthy weight, feel energetic, and stay on the path of good health. And as you'll soon learn in this book, the benefits of a plant-based diet extend to the environment. Eating meat accounts for more greenhouse gasses than all transportation worldwide. In fact, Worldwatch Institute has found that eating animals and their byproducts accounts for 51% of global warming. We also lose more land space and resources by supporting the livestock industry—animals that we "grow" to eat consume seven times more grain than the entire U.S. population!

Think how much land we could save, and how many hungry mouths we could feed, with all of that food and perhaps most importantly, how many animals' lives we could spare by moving to a plant-based diet. Putting plants on your plate won't just benefit you, but also the planet and all who live here.

Sensational Salads to Cool the Earth is a perfect addition to any kitchen, whether you're just starting your plant-based journey or you're well versed in vegan eating. I hope you enjoy all the valuable advice and fabulous recipes Ms. Love has waiting for you, and that you can invite others into your own kitchen to cook and share some of her nourishing salads together.

Introduction

HOW CAN A SALAD COOL THE EARTH?

If you are a curious person, you may have a question in your mind about the final phrase in my title, *Sensational Salads to Cool the Earth.* You may be wondering if my reference is to the kitchen cooling effect when we make an uncooked salad instead of turning on the oven or stove to make cooked food. Perhaps you assume I am optimistic or naïve enough to think that the cumulative effect of many people around the world making raw salads instead of cooked food could ultimately bring down the temperature of the whole earth. Well, I am certainly an optimist, and I do believe that the accumulated impact of many small acts does add up to significant change. That principle drives my assertion that salads can, indeed, cool the earth, but not by keeping the kitchen cool! Many of the salads in this book are raw and/ or uncooked; however there are also multiple recipes that will significantly heat up your kitchen.

No, my reference is not to the temperature in your kitchen, but to the crucial fact that there is not a single ingredient of animal origin in any of the recipes in this book. Although there is still a tremendous dearth of common knowledge and perhaps even more denial about the impact of animal agriculture on the environment, there is a strong and growing body of evidence implicating animal agriculture in climate change and most of the other pressing environmental challenges of our times. It is clear that our continued existence on a livable planet is reliant on the extent to which we collectively emphasize plants and minimize animal products in our diets. This book and the others in the *Tastes Like Love* series are dedicated to the proposition that as a society we can avert the environmental disasters associated with animal agriculture without sacrificing flavor or enjoyment. Since you are reading this book, I know you are partnering with me in this endeavor, or at least considering this, and I thank you!

WHAT'S UP WITH "TASTES LIKE LOVE?"

The first of my guiding principles for creating fabulous food is "energy has a taste."This principle acknowledges that the energy with which we prepare food infuses the end product with that taste. For example, if we are angry or resentful while preparing food, the taste of that rage or bitterness will be apparent to those who consume it. Similarly, if we are joy-filled during meal prep, that joy will radiate out from the food and fill every bite with light. I am fond of the taste of love that comes through so beautifully when I hold the energy of love while engaged in culinary activities. If you try this technique, I believe you too will find that your food tastes like love!

WHY SALAD?

Anyone who knows me, even a little bit, would probably agree that I am a huge fan of vegetables! Don't get me wrong, I also love fruit, grains, legumes, nuts, and seeds, but vegetables are dearest to my heart because they are full of phytonutrients, fiber and deliciousness! My body feels uber-energized when I eat my fresh veggies. Vegetables are non-controversially healthy, and by this I mean that I am unaware of any valid nutritional approach that finds fault with vegetables as a whole. I am a firm believer that it is impossible to eat too many vegetables. And salads are a wonderful way to consume vegetables. Salads provide endless amazingly rich and varied possibilities for combining vegetables and possible additions from other food groups plus a dressing bursting with flavor. Salads can be an essential side dish to any meal and can also dazzle as a meal unto themselves.

THE RECIPES

There are fifty recipes in this book, forty-one tasty nutritious salads, mostly with dressings, and nine additional dressing recipes. Every dish is wholesome, nourishing, plant-based, gluten-free, and scrumptious! Some of the recipes are entirely raw, living foods, and some include cooked foods. Because I love to use mostly locally or regionally sourced ingredients, the ingredients in each salad utilize fresh plant foods typically available at the same time of year where I live in Santa Cruz, California.

What you will not find in the recipes in this book are concoctions composed of heavily processed vegan imitation meat and dairy products. You will also not find many canned or frozen foods, or many foods typically sold in a package. The food is whole food, made from scratch. Nevertheless, I make use of various techniques, such as the wide use of pre-washed baby greens, to help you get many of the recipes on the table in a timely manner. The food is nourishing on a deep level, designed to be made with love. Some of the recipes in the book can take some time to cook, and would be best made when you feel like taking on a fun but lengthy process. That said, I believe this style of whole foods cooking can fit into a super active lifestyle, and I have proved that for myself for many years. To support you in fitting these recipes into your life, I include ideas for balancing a full life and food preparation from scratch in Section 1. Also included with some recipes are a variation called Meals on the Table Now, in which I offer suggestions for adapting the recipes to create delicious, satisfying, healthy meals in 15–25 minutes.

STRUCTURE OF THE BOOK

This book contains three sections. Section 1, "Celebrate Plants," includes information, encouragement, and ideas to support an increase in plant consumption. I also include a list of six guiding principles for making your food fabulously tasty.

Section 2, "The Recipes," is obviously where you will find the recipes! Additionally, I include notes, ingredient substitution suggestions, and variations (including the Meal on the Table Now variations) with most of the recipes.

Section 3 contains "Additional Resources" to support your food preparation experience. I include an ingredient glossary, additional recipes for some of the ingredients in the recipes, and a list of helpful resources that support plant consumption.

I am so excited to share these recipes and other tools and information with you! I am taking my own advice and infusing this book with the energy of love, trusting the book will be just as delicious as the food. Please let me know what recipes you make from this book and how the food turns out. I'd also love to hear if this book helps you to eat more plants and less animal products. Together we can increase vitality and compassion. Together we can cool the planet by eating our veggies, while simultaneously savoring the taste of love!

Celebrate Plants

Eat Your Veggies!

MAKE FRIENDS WITH PLANT FOODS

Are you a committed omnivore who is interested in really good food and perhaps wanting to do more for the planet and your health? Are you considering embarking on the journey into veganism? Or are you already vegan but interested in increasing your health and vitality or having more delightful taste sensations? Wherever you are on the continuum, you can't go wrong when you eat your veggies!

Vegetables and other plant foods are, in fact, the anchor of any healthy diet. I cannot say enough about how wonderful vegetables and fruits are when grown and prepared well. A whole foods vegan diet also typically includes nuts, seeds, whole grains and legumes, but in my book, veggies and fruits are the stars! This section provides story, inspiration, facts, encouragement, and resources to support you in eating more vegetables, fruits, and other plant-based foods.

My Story, or What Drove Me to Write This Book

I am a very passionate person. I am passionate about life, passionate about health, passionate about the children of the world, passionate about the earth, and especially passionate about creating delicious food that is an expression of these other passions! I will admit that my fervor for creating delectable food for people borders on obsession at times. As compulsions go, it is not only a fairly benign one, but potentially very helpful. That promise is the impetus for this book and the series of which it is a part. I will admit my bias right here: I believe that a plant-based lifestyle is the most impactful choice an individual can make to improve her/his health, express respect for all life, and contribute to sustainability of the earth and her resources. Yet the choice to embrace veganism is not a choice that everyone will make. While I hope that current vegans will find inspiration and encouragement in this book, I am primarily creating this book as a resource for omnivores. My intent is to encourage increased consumption of plants and decreased consumption of meat and dairy products as a way to contribute to a world in which all lifekind can thrive.

CHILDHOOD INFLUENCE

My own voyage to a committed vegan lifestyle began in my childhood, when my mother joined the "health nut" craze of the late 1960s and early 1970s and began a process of eliminating some foods from our family's diet and substituting other foods. As I recall, first we lost the red meat and the white sugar. Then the white flour was out, along with other refined grains like white rice. We also began avoiding food colors and artificial flavors as well as ingredients we could not pronounce or understand. Soon the rest of the meats followed, along with other processed foods. We added in whole grains, less refined sweeteners such as honey, and lots of legumes, nuts, and seeds. We also began eating more dairy products than we had previously, especially cheese and yogurt, if I recall correctly.

The whole family was converted to a vegetarian, whole foods diet by the early 1970s. Because the motivation for this change was improved health, that focus drove my continued commitment to vegetarianism as an adult, many years after my mother and most of the rest of the family resumed eating meat.

In addition to the health benefits, I thought my choice of vegetarianism was kind to animals because no one was being killed for my dinner, as far as I knew. I was eating a lot of dairy, but I was unaware of the terrible abuses of the dairy industry and was not looking to find out. I had given up eggs in my teen years, so I was a practicing lacto-vegetarian. I was content, maybe even smug, as a vegetarian, even though there was plenty of visceral evidence that dairy was not good for my health. I might have gone to my grave as an apologist for dairy, were it not for a fateful series of events that happened in the late 1980s.

A TURNING POINT

It was during that time period, in 1988, that I entered recovery to heal from my traumatic childhood. The conversion to vegetarianism was only one aspect of my childhood, an aspect I now see as one of the most useful things to keep. I had begun participating in a twelve-step recovery fellowship known as Co-Dependents Anonymous. In that fellowship, as in other twelve-step programs, there is a series of practical steps for transforming one's life. The third step is a doozy for people like me who like to be in control of our lives: "Made a decision to turn our will and lives over to the care of God as we understood God." I was a person who had experienced abuses of power throughout my life; therefore the thought of turning my will and my life over to another entity was intensely frightening. This was especially the case given my conception of God at that time, something outside of myself, much more powerful than me, and perhaps punitive or at least uncaring. What would God do with my life if I gave God control?

I had been in the program long enough, however, to have experienced relief and hope from working the first two steps. Additionally, I trusted the powerful testimonials of the many members who had longevity in the program and more experience in working the steps. So I made a decision to turn my life and will over to God. Suddenly I was seized with terror! For some reason, when I made that decision I became overcome with the fear that God would make me eat meat! I shared this thought with some of my twelve-step friends, and nobody thought God would do that. It did not make any sense. Still, I could not shake this fear. I had been a proud vegetarian for a decade and a half at that point and I did not want to put any meat in my body!

The crisis was resolved after an incident in which I was taking a walk down a main street in the town where I lived. There was a sidewalk sale that day and many shops had wares for sale outside their establishments. As I walked past a bookstore and scooted around some full bookshelves on the sidewalk, a book fell out of one of the shelves directly in front of my feet. The book? *The Higher Taste: A Guide to Gourmet Vegetarian Cooking and a Karma-Free Diet.* I was intrigued by the words "karma-free diet" and I certainly was amazed that the book volunteered to meet me! I bought the book and took it home to read.

TRANSFORMATION IN UNDERSTANDING

That was the catalyst for a transformation in my understanding and commitment that ultimately resulted in my entry into veganism. I no longer have the book, but I remember what I read that simultaneously helped me understand my fear about God and pointed a way forward that was more aligned with the new me. It was a statement to the effect that a vegetarian diet was karma-free, given the choice to avoid meat was driven by a desire to avoid harming others for one's pleasure. That resonated with me on some level, even though I did not embrace the full Hare Krishna theology in which this idea was embedded. My vegetarianism, previously committed to the cause of keeping me healthy (and perhaps unconsciously driven by a desire to be a little superior to those who ate meat), became transformed into a vehicle for realizing my spiritual intent to respect all life and to do no harm in pursuit of my pleasure. I came into the full realization that my vegetarianism had previously been dedicated to my ego, and it was this orientation that God might want me to release, not the practice of eschewing meat. The fear dropped away and I was able to fully embrace the beauty of the third step, with a nascent understanding that the God to whom I was turning over my will and life was benevolent and supportive of my healing.

I continued eating dairy, but began educating myself about agricultural practices to avoid supporting cruelty, given my new focus on doing no harm. Ultimately that led to the elimination of dairy and honey, and to non-dietary choices I continue to refine expressly for the purpose of respecting all life and reducing harm to the greatest extent possible. I continue to benefit in many ways from my vegan lifestyle; for instance I am renowned for my incredible energy. I rarely get any kind of illness. I feel great almost all of the time. I feel a sense of peace, knowing that I am doing my part to promote kindness to all beings. Finally, I know that my dietary choice is the most environmentally sustainable choice I can make, and is the largest individual contribution possible for countering human-caused climate change.

IMPETUS FOR ACTIVISM

It is these last benefits that have provoked a more recent and urgent impetus for vegan activism, including writing and publishing this book series to support people who want to make the change and provide confirmed meat-eaters with delicious options for eating more plants. For many years I have been content to do stealth vegan activism by feeding people amazing food as a way to demonstrate that no sacrifice in flavor is necessary when eating vegan food. This has been a pretty successful strategy to some degree, as the delight of the food has encouraged a number of people to eliminate or at least reduce their consumption of meat and dairy. I recently watched a movie that inspired me to take my activism to the next level, however.

The movie *Cowspiracy* is a must watch for everyone, in my opinion. The film raises the question of why animal agriculture, the leading cause of human-caused climate change, deforestation, habitat loss and so many other forms of environmental degradation, is not being addressed by the largest environmental organizations. I don't know if the question is completely answered in the movie, but I do know that the topic of meat eating is a sacred cow that most people, even staunch environmentalists, do not want to touch. I myself have been guilty of tippy-toeing around the subject in order to avoid offending people.

Watching the movie was a turning point for me, in that it reinforced my understanding that perhaps the only strategy that has the potential to successfully turn around the current pattern of human-caused environmental destruction is a mass human shift in dietary patterns. One of the most frightening environmental challenges we are facing is climate change. Although most of the political and community conversations about addressing climate change focus on reductions in carbon emissions, for example through greener transportation, the greenhouse gases produced by animal agriculture contribute more to global warming than all transportation combined.[1] The hopeful news, though, is that these potent climate forcers leave the atmosphere more quickly than carbon dioxide. Although it is not clear that reductions in carbon emissions will make a difference in time to avert the horrific consequences of climate change,[2] we do have the power to turn around global warming, to make a choice that will cool rather than warm the planet. That choice is to eat more plants and few or no animal products.

A MOMENT OF HIGH RESOLVE[3]

Shortly after watching *Cowspiracy* I experienced a moment of high resolve. My husband Golden Love and I were enjoying a meal together, and he began speaking philosophically as he often does, in this case offering appreciation for my life-long work with children and families, saying that I was tuned into the big idea that can save humanity, that of raising children in ways that are conducive to peaceful, harmonious relationships interpersonally and globally as a way to alter our human experience on the planet. I noticed I was feeling impatient with his effusive words of support. Suddenly I blurted out, "but what if there is no habitable planet for our children to inherit? Then it won't make any difference how we raise them." It was at this moment that I became clear that for the remaining years of my life I will work more openly for the cause of a habitable planet, while simultaneously continuing my activism for young people.

The argument I made to myself is very simple: given that we need our planet to be habitable in order to continue living on it, and given this requires us to effectively address climate change, and soon, I must do my part to respond to the life-or-death demand to promote a major change in human dietary patterns. This demand gives me the courage to push through my fears of offending people. This demand inspires me to be "out" about my enthusiastic participation in the movement of support for an inevitable shift away from excessive human meat and dairy consumption and toward a plant-based diet, a human diet that can be sustained for the billions of people and other creatures who are living on this planet. I pray that this book and the others to follow in the *Tastes Like Love* series contribute to that movement.

Five Urgent Reasons to Eat More Plants

You have already learned about my passion for plant eating by reading the Introduction and the previous chapter. In this section I will give more specific information about the reasons to do so. I want to start by acknowledging that some readers of this book may experience anger, disbelief, resistance, or judgment in response to some of my statements. You may disagree with my conclusions or doubt the veracity of the statistics and examples I offer. You may be a committed locavore or a person who has addressed a health challenge by eating meat or eggs. Or you may have a religious or cultural belief that animals are here for our use and consumption.

I want you to know that I have done my best to find studies that are well designed and apparently untainted by commercial sponsorship that reflects my bias. Where wide variations in data exist from study to study, I have chosen to present data that falls in the middle of the spectrum, or is conservative, or sourced from the meat industry itself. I am building a case, of course, but my intent is to use data justly in the process of building the case. Nevertheless I feel a sense of risk by going into this territory knowing that I am poking holes in sacred cows (mixed metaphor intended). And yet I feel compelled to do my part to encourage plant eating and discourage excessive consumption of animal products. If you are one of the people who experiences offense from my words, I hope that you will simply take what you like and leave the rest!

HEALTH

Did you know that heart disease is the number one killer in the U.S., followed closely by cancer?[4] According to the U.S. Centers for Disease Control and Prevention, approximately 600,000 people died of each of these diseases in 2014. Stroke, diabetes, and Alzheimer's disease are also in the CDC's top ten killer list. All are preventable and related to lifestyle choices. Research has demonstrated that a plant-based diet is a powerful way to prevent and even reverse these ailments, other chronic fatal diseases, and a number of risk factors for disease.

Let's look at heart disease, since it's the number one killer. Researchers offered 198 patients with cardiovascular disease a nutritional program that encouraged the elimination of animal products and added oils. Of the 89% of patients who complied with the dietary guidelines, 81% experienced improvement in their symptoms, and 22% experienced a complete reversal of their heart disease![5] Another study examined the diets and long-term health status of over 44,000 people and found that vegetarians had a 32% reduced risk of hospitalization and death due to heart disease, as compared with their meat-eating counterparts.[6]

There is also ample compelling evidence of the benefits of a plant-based diet in preventing cancer. One group of researchers looked at the diets of over 90,000 women and concluded that those who ate a plant-based diet had a 15% reduced risk of all forms of breast cancer, and a 34% decreased risk for one particular type of breast cancer.[7] Other researchers have found that a vegan diet results in a 35% reduced risk of prostate cancer compared to other types of diets,[8] that vegan diets confer a reduced risk for all cancers[9] and for female-specific cancers,[10] and that both a high-fiber, low fat diet[11] and increased consumption of legumes decrease the risk of colorectal cancer.[12]

Additionally, numerous research studies have demonstrated the efficacy of a plant-based diet in preventing and even reversing the symptoms of diabetes,[13] promoting weight-loss and reducing risk of obesity,[14] and promoting a healthy gut microbiome, thereby reducing the risk of disease.[15] One study demonstrated that a low-fat plant-based diet results in longer telomeres, the bits of DNA that protect the ends of our chromosomes and are associated with younger biological age and longer lives.[16]

Even increasing plant consumption without going all the way to veganism confers health benefits, according to multiple studies. For instance, high consumption of plant foods such as vegetables, fruits, and legumes is associated with a reduced risk for hip fractures,[17] feeling calmer and happier,[18] and remaining disease-free later in life.[19] Your brain can also benefit by eating more plant foods. People who consume the most fruits, vegetables, and whole grains demonstrated a reduced risk of cognitive decline[20] and Alzheimer's.[21] And older adults with the highest consumption of green leafy vegetables and cruciferous vegetables showed the lowest rates of cognitive decline in another study.[22]

These are merely statistics, however, and raw data may not be that persuasive.

What is compelling is the human experience behind this data. I'm sure you and everyone else reading this book knows at least one person who is struggling with obesity, Type 2 diabetes, heart disease, cancer, or other diet-related preventable diseases. Most of us have even lost loved ones to these diseases.

When I think about the fact that 17% of children in the U.S. are obese,[23] or that rates of childhood Type 2 diabetes, once rare, are skyrocketing,[24] or that hypertension is rising among children,[25] even though these are just data, I know that there are real human children behind the facts, real human families experiencing major disruptions in their lives. If even a percentage of these children recovered their health through dietary changes, wouldn't the work to make that happen be worth it?

ENVIRONMENT

As I mentioned in the Introduction, animal agriculture is a major driver of many of our most dire environmental threats. I will touch on a few of the issues here, and would highly encourage you to do some research on your own if this is a topic of interest to you. One of the fundamental reasons that animal agriculture is so destructive to the environment is that raising animals for food is a very resource-intensive proposition. Animals being grown for food and the plants to feed them occupy about 30% of the world's total land surface![26] Much of that is pasture, but 33% of global land fit for growing crops is being used to grow feed for animals.[27] Unfortunately, feeding those food crops to animals instead of people equates to a significant loss of human food realized per acre of land. It takes 10.8 pounds of grain to produce one pound of beef,[28] for example, according to a beef industry group. (Other sources give much higher figures.[29])

To illustrate the food loss from feeding the grain to animals instead of people, let's use the beef group's conservative feed conversion ratio, and corn, one of the most common grains fed to livestock. If you took the 10.8 pounds of corn that are required to produce a pound of beef, and instead of feeding it to an animal you made food for humans with it, you could make over 7.5 gallons of cooked hominy[30] or 235 tortillas![31] Given that our arable land globally is finite and our human population is growing, doesn't it make sense to feed the grain directly to humans?

Water is another resource of great concern, especially where I live in California. Animal agriculture consumes a tremendous amount of water in my state and worldwide. In fact an article in Scientific American states: "meat consumption accounts for 30 percent of the U.S. water footprint."[32] Yet at the height of the drought in California a couple of years ago, there was a significant outbreak in the press and social media of stories about the water consumption of another of California's crops: almonds.[33] Most of the stories declared that it takes 1.1 gallons of water to produce one almond, a figure that made almonds seem like a luxury that the earth cannot afford. The water requirements of other plant food crops were also included in some of the articles, but the almond was the big focus of attention. What was very interesting was the lack of even a mention in many of the articles about the real water guzzlers: animals being raised for food.

The production of animal products uses an incredibly disproportionate share of water when all of the inputs are included in calculations,[34] though specific figures vary widely. Using a fairly conservative figure, I can confidently say that it takes about 1,800 gallons of water to produce one pound of beef.[35] That means we could grow about 409 almonds with the same amount of water that it would take to grow the meat in a quarter pound hamburger. Do you know what 409 almonds looks like? Well, with approximately 92 almonds per cup,[36] you would get almost four and a half cups of almonds for the same water as that quarter pounder! While many people would think nothing of chowing down one or two quarter-pound burgers in a single meal, I don't know anyone who could eat more than a quart of almonds in one sitting! In fact one of the recipes for which I am most known, Tangy Dill Collard Wraps, uses one cup of almonds to make enough wraps for 6–8 people, so the water saved from foregoing that one burger would feed over two dozen people.

Inputs are only one side of the equation when it comes to environmental impacts. The outputs of animal agriculture are also disturbing. A staff report from the U.S. General Accounting Office says that farmed animals in the U.S. produce about 130 times more waste than humans in our country do, or about five tons of waste per year for each human citizen![37] Pollution from this waste makes its way into the land and water in the form of heavy metals, bacterial and viral pathogens, parasites, pharmaceuticals, detergents, disinfectants, and excess nitrogen and organic matter.[38] In addition to fouling the environment, ultimately these pollutants enter the bodies of human and non-human animals alike. Problems associated with these pollutants include destruction of aquatic environments, suppression of aquatic species, endocrine disruption, antibiotic resistance, developmental and neurological abnormalities, and diseases contracted via water-borne pathogens.[39]

Perhaps the most alarming outputs of animal agriculture, however, are the copious amounts of extremely potent greenhouse gases released in the process of producing meat, eggs, and dairy for the plates of consumers. Reducing consumption of these products, or going all the way to veganism, could result in significant reductions in an individual's contribution to climate change. One study calculated the output of diet-related greenhouse gases using consumption data from over 55,000 participants.[40] The vegans had the least impact, with diets that produced 2.89 kilograms of carbon dioxide equivalents per day. The "high meat eaters," on the other end of the spectrum, produced more than twice as much greenhouse gases with a carbon dioxide equivalent of 7.19 kilograms per day. Eliminating meat but not dairy and eggs put lacto-ovo vegetarians at 3.81. Even reducing one's meat intake made a difference, with "low meat eaters" at 4.67.

Reducing red meat and dairy products also appears to be a more effective strategy than being a committed locavore. One study analyzed total greenhouse gas emissions over the entire lifecycle for a broad array of foods. Included were emissions from production, distribution, and transportation. The researchers concluded, among other things, that "shifting less than one day per week's worth of calories from red meat and dairy products to chicken, fish, eggs, or a vegetable-based diet achieves more GHG [greenhouse gas] reduction than buying all locally sourced food."[41]

As with many topics, there are different opinions about the precise figures for greenhouse gas emissions from animal agriculture, and numerous complexities confound the situation. Nevertheless it is clear that animal agriculture makes a significant contribution. The Food and Agriculture Organization of the United Nations (FAO) produced one of the most quoted and comprehensive studies on the topic. The study concluded that animal agriculture is the source of 18% of global greenhouse gas emissions, a larger share than all transportation combined![42] This is alarming enough, yet it is far from the highest figure put forth by competent scientists. For example, two researchers enumerated multiple sources of greenhouse gases associated with animal agriculture but overlooked or intentionally omitted from the FAO report. For example, these researchers include greenhouse gases emitted from deforestation through burning for the purpose of clearing land for meat production.[43] They also utilize more up-to-date figures for number of livestock and tonnage of animal products produced. Their conclusion? That livestock account for 51% of global greenhouse gas emissions.[44]

Regardless of which methodologies one embraces, one thing that is crucial to understand is that there is tremendous variation between one greenhouse gas and another in terms of their global warming potential. Animal agriculture does contribute to global warming through carbon dioxide emissions. That is only part of the picture, however, as other gases released as part of the industry are far more potent than carbon dioxide in their warming potential. For example, methane has seventy-two times the warming potential as an equivalent amount of carbon dioxide.[45] According to the Environmental Protection Agency, the average passenger car releases 4.7 metric tons of carbon dioxide per year.[46] In a separate report, the same agency lists the methane production of cattle in the U.S. by type and region. For example dairy cattle in my state of California release 208 kilograms of methane per head per day,[47] which works out to 75.92 metric tons per year. That is already a whole lot more greenhouse gas released than the average passenger car, but when you factor in the 72:1 warming potential, that one cow in California has contributed the same amount of warming to the earth as would 5,466 metric tons of carbon dioxide, well over 1000 times more warming than the car![48]

Other greenhouse gases associated with animal agriculture also demonstrate greater warming potential than does CO2. The global warming potential of nitrous oxide, for example is 298 times that of CO2; 65% of the human-caused nitrous oxide in the atmosphere is from animal agriculture.[49] Black carbon, also called black soot, is even more potent, with about 1,000–4,000 times as much global warming potential as carbon dioxide.[50] Black soot comes from the incomplete burning of fossil fuels and organic matter, and in animal agriculture is primarily associated with the burning of forests to clear land for pasture.[51] The practice of clearing forests for pasture is also a cause of some of the other sad impacts of animal agriculture: deforestation, threats to biodiversity, and species extinction.

There is some hopeful news, though, as several greenhouse gases released in significant quantities by animal agriculture leave the atmosphere much more quickly than does CO2. Carbon dioxide remains in the atmosphere for hundreds or even thousands of years, whereas nitrous oxide is dissipated in 114 years, methane leaves the atmosphere in about 12 years, and black soot is very transient, with each particle lasting only a few days to a few weeks.[52] While it is doubtful that any reduction in carbon dioxide emissions will be sufficient to turn around global warming in time, reducing the sources of these shorter-lived climate forcers can have a significant impact on climate change. A number of studies have modeled the effects of population-wide replacements of some dietary animal products with plant foods and have demonstrated the tremendous power of such a shift in turning around climate change.[53] Each of us has the capacity to make a significant difference with our food choices. I think that's pretty empowering!

FOOD JUSTICE

According to the Food and Agriculture Organization of the United Nations (FAO), about 795 million people in the world are undernourished.[54] Food justice would entail finding a way to eat that is sustainable for everyone on the planet.

It may seem as though my food choices here in Santa Cruz, California could not possibly affect the experience of a person living in Sub-Saharan Africa, or any other region where hunger and starvation are facts of life for hundreds of thousands of people. Consider though, that, according to Dr. Richard Oppenlander, author of Food Choice and Sustainability and Comfortably Unaware, "82% of the world's starving children live in countries where food is fed to animals that are then killed and eaten by more well off individuals in developed countries like the US, UK, and in Europe."[55] Dr. Oppenlander further explains that a quarter of grain grown in developing nations is fed to livestock. Imagine the reduction in human hunger that would result from feeding the grain to the hungry people who are growing it rather than converting it at a huge loss into animal products for the developed world!

The situation is currently very dire for people living in poverty and not getting enough to eat. Given that the human population on our finite earth is growing, and the demand for animal products is also growing,[56] if our intent is food justice, the current trend is taking us in entirely the wrong direction. The most environmentally sustainable way to make sure that all can be fed is to emphasize plant foods that can be grown with much higher returns on all resources used and with outputs that ensure our planet continues to be habitable. If we all do our part by reducing consumption of animal products to the extent that we can, we can make sure that everyone is fed.

ETHICAL/SPIRITUAL:

When I was a child, maybe 10 or 11 years old, and several years before the advent of vegetarianism in my family, our father took my sister and brother and me out on a fishing expedition. If I remember correctly, he chartered a boat and we went out on the sea. Much of the experience is lost in the depths of memory, but I do clearly recall that I was the only person who caught a fish, a very large tuna. I also remember the sound of the fish after it had been hauled into the boat, disconnected from the hook, and placed into a wooden box on the deck; in fact this sound is the crispest part of the memory. For the rest of that expedition, until it finally died, the fish flopped around in the box, causing crashing, erratic, drumlike sounds. I was fixated on those sounds. They forcefully drove me to face the fact that I was the instigator of the slow, painful death of a living creature. If, as seems likely, there was blood in the box when the fish was removed, or if the body of the fish was lacerated from its heroic struggles, I have completely blocked these things out of my memory.

In recalling the incident, I want to believe that I begged and pleaded with my father to let the fish go. I can almost see my child self doing that, hear myself crying out for mercy for the fish. I even seem to have a vague recollection of my dad taking a stubborn stand; after all, he had paid good money to charter the boat for the purpose of catching fish! In actuality, however, I don't really know if I even made the suggestion that the fish be released. I may have simply sat, silent and numb, feeling disempowered to right the wrong that I had surely just committed.

I also want to believe that I took a stand when my Baba (Dad's mother) cooked the fish and served it to us later that day. I want to believe that I refused to eat it and that I made my reasons clear. But I don't really know whether I ate it or not, or whether I said anything or not.

I fantasize about the idea of having had that incident be a conversion experience—of having sworn off of eating living creatures ever after. I know that that did not happen.

How is it that most of us who live in cultures in which the eating of meat is normalized become so shut off from the ethical and spiritual dimensions of routine cruelty and killing? How have we, as a species, so fully otherized our animal brothers and sisters such that we can take their bloody, dead bodies into our bodies for pleasure without even giving it a second thought? How can we tolerate the ripping of children away from their mothers in order that we might enjoy the mothers' milk? Or the excruciatingly horrifying realities of imprisoning animals in Auschwitz-style conditions so we can take pleasure from consuming their body parts, their children, their potential children?

In my experience, enculturation is a very strong contributor to beliefs and behaviors. We humans are social creatures, and in our early years we learn what it means to be human by observing and mimicking those around us. This process happens so automatically and at such an early age, that most of us don't think to question the underlying assumptions of the various practices we receive and embody. What I know is that we can begin to raise questions, regardless of how long we have individually or collectively been engaging in a particular pattern of behavior. And I know that our questioning can result in new decisions, new practices, and even great change in the world, when enough of us act together.

Today there are many people who do care about the well-being of animals and who want to support a more compassionate approach. This is evidenced by the rise in consumption of foods labeled with such names as "sustainable," "organic," "cage-free," "free-range," and "grass fed." Whether a person identifies as spiritual or religious or not, it just feels better to live in the world in a way that is compassionate and caring. If you are a person who wants to be vegan as a way of expressing your care for all beings but has struggled to make the shift, I encourage you to get the support, tools, and inspiration you need to realize your highest commitment. If you are a person who eats animal products and wants to continue doing so, but want to reduce harm and bring your practices into greater alignment with your values, I encourage you to do the research so you will be fully informed as to the practices on the farms with which you do business. It is easier in some ways to stay in the dark, but the warm glow of the light is ultimately more satisfying.

I want to acknowledge that the path of compassion is a journey in which the goal of doing no harm will never be reached. With the best of intentions and highest of resolves, we can still do harm. Perhaps I unknowingly buy a plant-based food that was processed by human workers who are subjected to inhumane conditions. Or I am experiencing a harried day and am not careful enough with some ants who have come into my kitchen. Even on days when I have maximum patience and an open heart, I most likely accidentally kill or maim small insects on my walk out to the garden. Cutting myself some slack is also part of the journey of compassion. For each of us, finding the balance of violence and nonviolence that meets our own comfort level is an important developmental task of life.

ECONOMIC

There are economic benefits to emphasizing plants in the diet as well. Perhaps the most obvious area for significant cost savings is the area of health care. The reduced cost for medical interventions for preventable dietary-related diseases is considerable. There are also tremendous environment-related cost benefits of a collective shift toward a plant-based or plant-rich diet. A group of researchers took on the task of analyzing the monetized costs of the health and environmental impacts of a number of different diets and published their work in the Proceedings of the National Academy of Sciences. Their findings? "Transitioning toward more plant-based diets…could reduce global mortality by 6–10% and food-related greenhouse gas emissions by 29–70% compared with a reference scenario in 2050.…Overall, we estimate the economic benefits…to be 1–31 trillion US dollars, which is equivalent to 0.4–13% of global gross domestic product (GDP) in 2050."[57] Pretty powerful, isn't it?

Plant-Consumption Fears, Myths, and Barriers

When I tell people that I am vegan, more than half of them respond with the same question, "How do you get your protein?" The smart aleck in me always wants to respond by saying something like, "Oh, you're a meat eater? How do you get your fiber?" But usually I refrain! Instead, I patiently explain that there is plenty of protein to be found in the vegetable kingdom, and that most people get too much, rather than too little protein. Have you ever met anyone suffering from kwashiorkor? That's the disease people get if they are deficient in protein, and it's extremely rare in the developed world or anywhere where people get enough food to eat.[58] It's so rare that I couldn't even find a figure on it, but I am certain that it is rarer than veganism by an order of many magnitudes!

The second most common response I hear is some variation of the following: "You have to be really careful to get all your nutrition on a vegan diet." Many people even refer to the idea that vegans have to very strategically combine amino acids from different food groups in each meal in order to get complete protein, an idea that was popular many decades ago, but which has long since been disproved.

When I meet parents or grandparents of young people who are embarking on plant-based diets, they are usually very concerned about their loved one. Typically they are fearful that their loved one will not get proper nourishment given that they are no longer eating animal products.

UNDERLYING IDEA

The idea underlying all these assumptions and fears is that a diet containing meat and dairy is inherently healthy. Therefore, eliminating these "healthy" foods results in a diet that is deficient, or at least potentially unhealthy, unless one takes extraordinary measures to replace nutrients assumed to be primarily available from animal products.

These ideas appear to be deeply embedded in the collective conscience, at least in the U.S. where I live, and probably in many other places as well. The science, however, does not back them up. As I mentioned in the section about eating plants for health, study after study demonstrates that eating more plants leads to greater health outcomes. In those studies that look at the health status of various populations segregated by diet, the vegans end up on top.[59] Eating more plants makes us healthier, and the counterpart is also true: eating more animal products is correlated with disease and early death in myriad studies. Yet the idea persists that meat, eggs, and dairy are healthy.

VEGAN FOOD: VARIED AND VIBRANT!

Two additional ideas I also hear frequently, especially from people who are interested in veganism but struggling to make the shift, is that vegan food is boring or that the food choices are extremely limited. If you relate to this idea, I encourage you to try the recipes in this book and see if you come to a different conclusion! What I experience as a vegan chef is endless possibilities of combinations of tasty vegetables, fruits, grains, legumes, nuts, seeds, herbs, and spices. Many of the best, most vital cuisines in the world emphasize plants and can easily be prepared without animal products. Consider the wide variety of Thai and Indian curries, Sri Lankan spicy potatoes or mushroom masala, Mexican bean burritos, Japanese seaweed salad, Ethiopian injera with piles of fragrant spice-laden vegetable dishes, Middle Eastern falafel and hummus spread, and the list goes on. Even "American" food can be made vegan, as the myriad varieties of veggie burgers can attest! In fact, there are very few world cuisines that cannot be made plant-based. What's boring or limited about that?

IS IT HARD?

Another misconception I frequently hear from people who learn I follow a plant-based diet is about how hard that must be. I acknowledge that there are places in the world where plant eating is so countercultural that there may be significant challenges. I also acknowledge the tremendous privilege I have living in Santa Cruz, California, where veganism is fairly common and there is an abundant supply of vegan food. Yet I have also been able to easily obtain vegetables, fruits, legumes, whole grains, nuts, and seeds in my travels in the U.S. and in the few other countries I have visited.

One thing to keep in mind is that supply follows demand. The supply of available choices increases as more and more people discover the benefits of eating plants and make requests at restaurants and grocery stores. If you live in an area that doesn't cater to plant eating well, make your needs known. Merchants want to make a sale, and they will respond if you are persistent. There are also many online venues for purchasing staples such as beans, grains, nuts, and seeds. A few of these are listed in the resource list in Section 3.

I don't mean to minimize the challenges people may face when making a commitment to change. There are a number of potential barriers that may need to be addressed and surmounted. This is especially the case for those who decide to make a complete shift to a vegan diet, but is also a potential for those who want to reduce animal consumption and increase plant eating.

ATTACHMENT

One very common barrier is human attachment. Let's face it—we get attached to things, whether they are good for us or not! I remember how difficult it was to give up dairy cheese, for example, even though it caused significant health challenges for me. I loved cheese so much that I actually organized a buying co-op to be able to obtain large quantities of cheese for a low cost. Cheese was an integral part of many of my most cherished and popular recipes. It was challenging to give up because I both loved the taste and had a close relationship with cheese. I later found out that there are addictive properties in it as well!

The good news is that addictions can be released and tastes can change. Getting through the initial shift can ultimately be met with a greater sense of ease, at least in my experience. When I walk through a cheese department at the grocery store now, the same smells that used to evoke mouth-watering pleasure now conjure up feelings of sadness as I think of the young calves being torn from their mothers and put in veal crates to satisfy the human desire for cheese. It isn't an appetizing feeling.

And I have learned to make delicious, nutritious, and satisfying plant-based cheeses that do not smell like cruelty. I think my former dairy cheese recipes taste even better now with the vegan cheeses. (An added benefit is I don't get the mucous coating in my mouth that I used to get from dairy cheese.)

INSPIRATION ABOUNDS

Another potential barrier to shifting is lack of information about what to eat on a plant-based diet. The good news is that inspiration abounds! Organizations like Physicians Committee for Responsible Medicine and Vegan Outreach offer such supports as tips, recipes, and menu plans to help with your transition to a plant-rich diet. The Internet, including social media, can be a great source of information, inspiration, and even support. For instance there is a thriving and supportive vegan community on Instagram offering up a mind-blowing constant stream of creative food ideas. One Green Planet (http://www.onegreenplanet.org/) is another great source for recipe ideas. Sign up to receive their newsletter and you will be amazed at the ideas delivered daily to your inbox!

There are also many excellent vegan cookbooks on the market. This is one area where I am choosing to make a contribution. I hope the recipes in this book and the other books to follow in the Tastes Like Love series will help you surmount the ideas barrier and unleash your creative plant-based genie!

JOIN THE COUNTERCULTURE

Finally, perhaps the most common barrier arises simply because at this time in history, in the U.S. and perhaps in most places in the world, animal-product consumption is the norm. Therefore, a choice to reduce or eliminate animal products is countercultural. People making the shift may find that their friends and loved ones have concerns and fears about the decision. They may find themselves having to defend their choice when people ask the inevitable questions about how they will get their protein or whether they know enough to get a balanced diet. They may experience pressure to come back into alignment with the norm.

It's one thing for me, vegetarian for over four decades and vegan for two, to have a facetious voice in my head with a snappy comeback about fiber, and another thing entirely for a newbie to deal with the fears, concerns, and lack of support of their loved ones.

I believe this is one of the biggest factors behind stories about people who tried to be vegan and failed. They tried to do something outside of the norm and did not get sufficient support for their choice. That's why I encourage anyone embarking on this path, whether going all the way to veganism or taking steps in that direction, to get support. Many areas have clubs or groups such as vegan meetups or Facebook groups where you can take your questions, give and receive support, and generally feel connected to a community of like-minded individuals. Another option is to look for a mentor. Many organizations also offer some form of support as well as information to help fortify one's choice. In the third section of this book I list a few organization I have found helpful.

Because I believe this need for support is so crucial, I have designed a program for people who are making the shift. I would love to hear from you if you are interested!

Your Process, Your Way

In the vegan movement, many people distinguish between eating a plant-based diet and being a vegan. I remember once I made a comment on a vegan online forum about people being vegan for different reasons, and a member of the group essentially called me out. She said that vegan equals justice and that someone on a plant-based diet is not necessarily a vegan. Her comment "vegan equals justice" references a commitment to justice for non-human animals. She was essentially saying that if a person is on a plant-based diet but is not committed to the movement to liberate animals from cruelty, that person is not a vegan. I appreciated the schooling.

I think of our dietary and lifestyle choices as points on an ever-evolving journey, rather than a destination. If you are looking to reap the harvest of health benefits available by eating plants, but aren't committed to animal rights, you may make different choices from those of a staunch activist. If you are concerned about the environment and want to drastically reduce your global warming contribution, but are not as concerned about the health impacts of diet, you may make yet a different choice. My point is that you are in the driver's seat and you are the navigator as well. You get to decide if your goal is to eliminate all animal products from your diet and your lifestyle, or to avoid certain products, or simply to make a reduction.

And I am pretty sure that your decision will change over time, especially if part of your commitment involves ongoing education. I have found that my choice not to cause harm in the pursuit of my own pleasure has had changing ramifications over time. Although I have identified as vegan for 20 or so years, what "vegan" means to me has morphed significantly over time, and those changes in meaning have provoked (or been provoked by) changes in my practices. My commitment means that I am not sticking my head in the sand; rather I am continuously learning, and as I learn I modify my choices. Grief is often a part of the process. Even as I know I am moving toward a greater sense of alignment, I experience human attachment and loss.

A CRUCIBLE FOR INCREASED COMPASSION

It turns out that these experiences of change, loss, grief, and realignment help me develop a greater sense of compassion for others who are making the choice to change. One recent experience helped me to reconsider the idea of sacrifice. I had been in the habit of saying that no sacrifice is necessary in the pursuit of a plant-based or plant-rich diet, and I really believed that was so. Then I had a sudden realization that it was time to release all of my silk clothing.

Because of the cruelties of the silk industry, I have not purchased any new silk in well over two decades. I still owned some things from my pre-vegan days, and I also was in the habit of buying silk clothing from thrift stores, reasoning that the original purchaser had supported the silk industry and I was supporting the recycling industry. Last spring I suddenly realized that I no longer had the stomach to put on any of the silk clothing. It was no longer a fit for my consciousness. The recycling story that had worked for so long abruptly stopped working.

On that day I piled up all my silk things on my bed. As I took each skirt, dress, shirt, scarf, or other article out of my closet and laid it in the pile I shed tears of loss. Eventually I was in deep, deep grief over a pile of clothes! I took a few photos to post the evidence of my shift on Facebook, then took the clothes to a garage sale that was being held for a nonprofit organization. As I released these clothes, some of which I had made myself and or had worn for important rites of passage, I realized that my earlier theory about sacrifice could not hold true for all people transitioning to a plant-based or plant-rich diet. My big sense of grief about the clothes reminded me to have more compassion for people who are giving up cheese, or bacon, or fish, or other apparent old friends in their efforts to align with their new consciousness.

So wherever you are on the continuum of plant eating, I hope you will give yourself the space and empathy you need to make your shift. It is your process, and you get to do it your way. Nurture yourself through feelings of loss. Be strong and be true to yourself. You can make a difference!

Six Guiding Principles For Fabulous Flavor

I have found that making delicious, nutritious food is a delightful and rewarding process. I don't like rules, because they can be arbitrary and by their very nature provoke insurgence from any rebellious soul. I stand by principles, however. To me, principles operate like laws of nature. There isn't any moral value in gravity working, nor is there a question about whether it will work or not; it just does. Following are some key guiding principles that I believe apply to food preparation and beyond. Making use of these principles in a conscious way will make the food taste better!

ENERGY HAS A TASTE.

Have you ever eaten food prepared by someone who was in a foul mood as they interacted with the food? Did it taste good? Or was it bitter or harsh tasting? How about the opposite? Have you eaten something that was prepared by someone who brought joyful energy to the task? How did that food taste? The energy with which we do anything permeates that thing with its nature. This is the most important principle to understand and embody in order to make tasty food or really to create anything that will have a positive impact in the world. Given that I know my energy cannot be hidden in the final product, but will be revealed for all to taste, I choose to infuse the food I prepare with the energy of love. And how does the energy of love taste? It *Tastes Like Love*!

ANYTHING WILL GIVE UP ITS SECRETS IF YOU LOVE IT ENOUGH.

This principle was stated by George Washington Carver and is a favorite of a former mentor of mine. If we love something, we pay attention to it. We are curious about it. We listen to it and we observe it. We take time to be present with it. We notice what is wonderful about it, and we offer appreciations. If we love it enough, we make a commitment to it, and we faithfully honor that commitment over time. When we find out disturbing or unsettling things about that which we love, we lean into our love for it so we can re-cultivate a sense of connection. Through this process of paying attention, being curious, listening and observing, taking time, being present, praising the good, making a commitment, and coming back to the love when we feel separate, we do learn so much about the object of our love. And by knowing our beloved more deeply and understanding its secrets, we are able to interact with it in effective ways that result in bounteous expressions of good.

I love preparing, serving, and eating delicious, nutritious food, and this love comes naturally to me. Because I love it, I pay attention to the vegetables, the herbs, the fruits. I understand little secrets that have come to me over time, so when I go to market I can select fruits and vegetables that taste the best. Because I love it, I take the time to be present, to smell, to feel, to intuit. Because I love it, I get curious. Will this taste good with that? Or with that? Because I love it, I notice and appreciate the delicious creations that come through. And because I love it, I feel inspired to share this love with others.

But what if one doesn't love food preparation, I hear some readers object! My suggestion is to start with willingness. Are you willing to learn to love food preparation? Declare your willingness! Are you open to the possibility? Cultivate that possibility by seeing your future self in pure delight as you create delicious nourishing dishes. Is there some small thing about food prep that you do love? Maybe you like to make smoothies in your blender or mash up an avocado for guacamole. Start with what you love and grow your love from there. Set your intention to learn to love food prep, and you will move in that direction. You will find that as you love it more, the food starts tasting better, and you will be carried into a delightful feedback loop in which love feeds more love. Through that increase of love, you too will learn the secrets of food prep and your food will demonstrate that knowing.

WE ARE ALWAYS AT CHOICE.

At every moment in time we have the capacity to make an infinite number of choices. We can choose to do what we did before, or some variation of it, or something entirely new. We may be out of touch with that choice, but it is always only a conscious thought away. This is as true for food preparation as for any other area of life. I see recipes as suggestions, inspiration, and options, not as dictates that must be followed rigidly. The recipes in this book are meant to be a starting point for your authentic creative expression. When you make choices to follow the guidance you receive because of the love you have for the food, you may stray significantly from the recipe as written. By paying attention to what you love, you will almost certainly notice that food tastes better when it is fresh and in season, for example. Therefore, if you are making a fruit salad that calls for apricots and when you go to the store discover that the apricots were grown in the other hemisphere and are hard with no fragrance, you will make a choice to substitute the delightful ripe pears that you started smelling the moment you walked into the produce department. You are always at choice and the recipes are a starting place. Be creative, flexible, spontaneous, and bold!

JUNK IN JUNK OUT.

This saying is often used to refer to data, but since it is a principle, it also applies to food preparation. My second most powerful secret for making food delicious, after "energy has a taste," is to use the freshest, highest-quality ingredients that I can find. When you are shopping for food or picking it from your garden, use as many senses as possible. Touch it, smell it, observe it, listen to it. Look for vegetables that are plump and tender rather than dried up and woody. Choose fruits that are fragrant and have good color. Learn the sounds of ripe melons. Learn the feel of young root crops. Grow or purchase and use fresh herbs, and lots of them. If you must use herbs out of season, consider freezing cubes of herbs when they are in season instead of using shriveled up old dried herbs! Buy whole spices in small quantities and grind what you need. Perk up a dish with a squeeze of fresh lemon or lime juice, not the kind that comes from a bottle. Use whole foods, minimally processed. Purchase organic food for the best flavor, sustainability, and health value. If something gets too old, find an alternate use for it rather than spoiling your good food with junk. For example you can use wilted or dried up produce in vegetable stock, or give it to your worms or your garden.

Starting with high-quality food gives you a great head start and is the first of my two part equation: "start with good food and don't wreck it." After you have taken the time to use your love and your choice to select fresh, whole, nutritious food, prepare it in ways that enhance and compliment the fresh, high quality food you have. A few tips for "not wrecking it" include serving most vegetables raw or lightly cooked, combining flavors that complement each other without putting too many different flavors in any one dish, and adding salt, salty condiments, and oils sparingly. Remember you can always add more of something but generally cannot take it out once added. When I'm creating in the kitchen I often have a tiny testing bowl in which I can put a spoonful of something and add an herb, spice, or other addition. Then I taste the dish to determine if my proposed addition will work well in it or not.

BLESSING FOOD HAS A TANGIBLE IMPACT ON ITS VITALITY.

I remember hearing many years ago about a study that demonstrated that blessing food before eating it results in a measurable, statistically-significant increase in nutrients. I don't know if the information I heard was correct, but I do know that significant research confirms that the regular practice of prayer confers health benefits on the person praying.[61] In the studies, the beliefs and specific practices of the person praying doesn't matter; the act of blessing has the same impact regardless of particularities. So I consider my household's communal practice of having a moment of silence followed by a verbal New Thought style prayer a suitable blessing, and I also consider my quick "Thank you for this delicious food" an appropriate prayer when I'm on the run. Words are not even necessary for it to be a blessing: sometimes it's enough just to breathe in the fragrance of the food for a moment with a feeling of gratitude in my heart. In my adult son's home, they bless each meal with a high five over the food, and I have no doubt that this blessing enhances the experience of eating as well.

One of the most powerful experiments I ever encountered regarding the act of blessing and its impact on the nutritional value of food involved some rabbits on a high cholesterol diet. As vegans, rabbits do not normally encounter cholesterol in their diet. This group of rabbits was being fed cholesterol as part of an experiment about heart disease. There was a surprise at the end of the study; one group of rabbits had not developed heart disease even though they had been fed the exact same diet as the others. It turned out that the person in charge of this healthy group of rabbits was petting and cuddling the rabbits and talking to them lovingly each time she fed them the toxic food. It seems that this act of "blessing" somehow created a different metabolic experience for the cuddled rabbits, an experience that resulted in vitality in spite of eating the same foods that were killing the other rabbits![62]

And while I have never seen studies about flavor improvements based on blessing, I absolutely believe it is true from my experience. The first time I experienced the difference that blessing could make on taste was when I was about 15 years old. My family was helping out a friend by selling a bunch of pumpkins he had grown. We would take a truckload of pumpkins into the center of a nearby town and sell them to people out of the back of the truck. One day we had a significant amount of pumpkins left when we were ready to go home. We gave them to a Hare Krishna group that was chanting in the park.

A few days later when we returned to the city where we had encountered the Hare Krishna devotees, we gratefully accepted the free meal they were offering, and part of the meal was the pumpkins. Now these were not Sugar Pie pumpkins. They were Halloween-style pumpkins that I had tried unsuccessfully to prepare for consumption in many ways. They just didn't taste good. On that day in the park with the Hare Krishnas, I found to my surprise that the pumpkin dish they served, made from the very pumpkins that had completely stumped my considerable culinary capacities, tasted absolutely delicious! When I asked the cook the secret, she put her index finger up in the air and said she had made the dish for that One and had given Him the first taste. That was a lesson I will always remember. So although I stand by the importance of selecting fresh produce with naturally-obtained deliciousness, when that is not possible the food can still be made whole with a blessing.

OUR THOUGHTS ARE CREATIVE.

The final principle for fabulous flavor is a truth that has been known and written about by sages and teachers from ancient times through today. This principle has many variations: "What you think about comes about," "Whatever you focus your attention on grows in your experience," "Thoughts become things," "Every idea in consciousness finds its corresponding expression in the physical world," "Cause and effect," etc. When I say that our thoughts are creative, I'm not talking about creativity in the artistic sense, though that can be true as well. What I am pointing out is that things that we experience and create in the world start out with thoughts. I cannot make a delightful five-course Asian California Fusion meal without starting with some idea in my mind. I cannot make endless varieties of nourishing salads or raw whole foods desserts or new flavors of live sauerkraut without first having an inspiration.

It is also true that I cannot make a spectacularly failed pot of soup or batch of muffins without first having this thought in mind! For example, on the few occasions on which I have made a dish or a meal that was truly awful, I can always trace the origins of that mess back to a thought or series of thoughts. Typically when this has happened, my ego was engaged in trying to impress a person or group and I started entertaining fears of disaster. Instead of moving my mind back to love and aligning my consciousness with the possibility of deliciousness, I have allowed my mind to fixate on the possibility of failure. I have worried and fretted, therefore infusing the food with the energy of worry, fret and fear. No wonder the food tasted less than spectacular!

I have proved this principle to myself so many times that I trust it implicitly. I encourage you to give it a try and see if your experience doesn't replicate mine. Just remember to discipline your mind, keeping your thoughts on the beautiful, powerfully nutritious, scrumptious food you are preparing, and hold a vision of it done. See yourself in joy as you nourish yourself and all life by preparing and consuming the fruits and veggies of the earth!

Eating Plants is Easy!

There are many ways to make plant eating the easiest and tastiest choice while staying healthy. It is also possible to balance whole foods meal preparation with a full life. Here are some of the tips I have discovered. Please let me know if you have additional ideas!

STOCK STAPLES

One helpful thing to make your plant-based meal prep easier is to make sure to keep basic staples well stocked so that you can easily create a meal with what's on hand. In my house, we love to have one, two, or more salads a day, so we make sure we have pre-washed baby greens in stock for quick salad prep. Other salad ingredients that are almost always available at The Love House are carrots, sprouts, avocado, sauerkraut, nuts, seeds, and smoked tofu. When it's lunchtime, it is easy to quickly throw together a salad and feel nourished and satisfied. Other staples we keep on hand include onions, garlic, fresh ginger, brown rice, various kinds of dried beans and lentils, quinoa, tofu, tempeh, tamari, olive oil, balsamic vinegar, coconut oil, rice cakes, tahini, nut butters, fresh in-season fruit, and whatever vegetables we find in the garden or at the farmers market. There is always something available to easily put together a meal.

START WITH INSPIRATION

I usually figure out the answer to the question, "What's for dinner?" by looking at the vegetables I have on hand in the garden or fridge. This technique provides inspiration for a meal that reflects the changing seasons and makes use of what I have.

CREATE LEFTOVERS AND "PLANNED OVERS"

Although I have been regularly preparing much more than we need for one meal for many years in order to have additional meals of the leftovers, my friend Beverly Boyd recently introduced me to the phrase "planned overs." Making a large pot of bean soup or vegetable stew or curry only takes a little longer than making a small pot, and nets you one or more additional meals that can very quickly be warmed and put on the table. Another technique is to make an abundance of roasted or steamed vegetables; eat some with your current meal and put some aside to toss into a salad the next day. Making a large pot of beans or grains and using it over several days in different variations is another planned-over practice. For example, you can make a large pot of garbanzo beans and use some the first day in a bean and veggie soup, then throw some onto a salad for lunch the next day, then turn the remainder into hummus on the third day.

Several of the salads in this book contain Meal on the Table Now variations that make use of the planned over concept. I also intentionally created recipes with large yields, in cases in which the salad keeps well. That way you can take a bountiful dish to a potluck or you can get more meals out of your prep time if eating at home. One note regarding salad planned overs: if a recipe calls for placing the salad mixture on a bed of greens and you have more salad than you will eat in one sitting, put away a portion to have on a subsequent day before adding greens.

USE SHORTCUT INGREDIENTS

Pre-washed baby greens are a boon for people with full lives. Getting sufficient green leafy vegetables into one's body is an important preventative health practice, yet the time needed to get them clean can be a deterrent to use. Many stores and farmers markets sell a variety of super nutritious greens in bulk or in packages, and these are generally pre-washed. If you grow your own greens, you can wash them after harvesting and before putting them in the fridge in order to shorten the food prep at mealtime.

Canned beans are another shortcut ingredient, but I have a word of caution. Commercially-available canned foods may contain trace amounts of the plastics that are used to line the cans. Many cans are lined with bisphenol A (BPA), a known endocrine disruptor. Unfortunately, even if you choose BPA-free cans, the replacement lining chemicals may be no healthier or safer than the BPA. I do recommend Eden brand beans. Their cans are lined with a plant-derived substance, oleoresin, rather than a plastic like BPA, BPB, vinyl, or polyester.

Other shortcut ingredients that can be used are pitted and sliced olives, instant wakame (which is precooked and dried), shelled nuts, and pre-toasted nori sheets. You can use shortcut ingredients but still make whole foods meals by avoiding overly processed shortcut foods like packaged or frozen meals.

UTILIZE TECHNIQUES FOR SPEED

There are a number of food prep techniques that reduce the time needed to make food. One such tip is to peel garlic by smashing it instead of painstakingly removing every tiny bit of skin by hand. If you cut the stem end off of each clove, then give it a strong whack with the side of the knife, the peel will be so loose as to easily slip off. Another speed tip involves stripping leaves off stems of herbs such as mint, basil, oregano, thyme, and rosemary, rather than carefully picking off each individual leaf. Grasp the herb stem with one hand close to the top but not so high that you are on a really tender spot. Using the other hand, pinch the stem below the holding hand, then rapidly pull downward, stripping the leaves off the stem. Pull the tender tip and leaves off the top as well. Kale and other leafy greens also respond well to this technique.

Learn to use a French chef's knife by rocking, rather than lifting. This motion will both speed up your process and also be easier on your muscles. Wash and take the stems off of bunches of cilantro, dill, or spinach by plunging the whole bunch in a bowl of clean water, then grasping the bunch above and below where you want the tear to be and twisting. Cut celery quickly by leaving the stalks attached. Run water inside to clean; then lay it out on a cutting board. Trim about a quarter of an inch off the tops of the stalks (if they appear dried out) and discard, then cut across the whole head of celery at whatever thickness you choose.

Save time when cutting long cylindrical vegetables like carrots and zucchini by laying two or more together next to each other on your cutting board and slicing them at the same time. With beans and peas you can cut across a much greater number of them at once. To slice grapes or cherry tomatoes in half quickly, place the flat of one hand over as many as you can cover, and slice horizontally through them with the knife in your other hand.

INCREASE AVAILABILITY OF TASTY INGREDIENTS

Even if you don't have a garden or space to grow a lot of food, consider growing a few strategically chosen herbs and/or vegetables in your yard, in containers on your patio, or even in pots in the house if you have enough light. If you only have room or capacity for a few things, I recommend an assortment of perennial herbs such as rosemary, oregano, sage, tarragon, and several types of thyme. It can be challenging to find fresh herbs at the store in some regions, and few things pack a flavor punch in such a small and healthy package better than fresh herbs do. If you live in a mild climate area, you will most likely be able to harvest perennial herbs all year long. In colder climates you can preserve some of the harvest by freezing (directions in Section 3).

Edible flowers are another lovely choice, as these can be very scarce in markets. If you have space, a few choice vegetable plants can also complement your culinary creations. Watermelon radishes are tasty and beautiful to look at, but rare in markets, so you might grow a few of these. Or maybe you would enjoy a greater variety of salad greens or cooking greens than are available for purchase. In our yard we have a tremendous variety of perennial and self-sowing annual greens such as red-veined sorrel, claytonia, lamb's quarters, purslane, tatsoi, arugula, tree collards, chickweed, nasturtium leaves, mustards, cress, and others. The variety of tastes, textures, and colors makes for a delightful salad that would not be achievable with the use of the limited palette of store-bought greens available in most areas.

CREATE YOUR OWN FLAVOR ADDITIONS

It is always wonderful to have tasty condiments on hand, and it is really special if they are homemade! You can learn to make such foods as sauerkraut, mango pickle, jalapeños en escabeche, hot sauce, umeboshi plums, nut cheeses and yogurts, etc. Look for upcoming books in the *Tastes Like Love* series that will have recipes and instructions for creating fermented foods and other homemade flavor powerhouses.

MAKE A SIMPLE MEAL

Select and make a simple salad from the book to be the centerpiece of your meal. Bring rice cakes or whole grain crackers and tahini or nut butter to the table. Provide table knives so people can spread their own crackers. Voila! You have a meal.

BE PLAYFUL

Everything is easier when it's fun! Make sure you bring the element of play into your food preparation. Even if it doesn't speed things up, you will be less aware of the passage of time if you are having a good time!

Color Outside of the Lines: Making this Book Fit for You

Following are a few suggestions for fully implementing one of the Six Principles for Fabulous Flavor: "We are always at choice." These are merely suggestions; I trust you will find other ways to color outside of the lines!

COMBINING

Have a salad meal by making two to five of the salads and eating them together; be creative about your combinations. Or mix and match dressings, for example by using the Shiitake Sesame Dressing from the Baby Spinach with Spicy Braised Tempeh on the Spinach Salad with Candied Pecans and Roasted Veggies. Or swap out greens, for instance using watercress with the Creamy Dilled Potato Kraut Salad or replacing the sprouts in the Lentil Quinoa Salad with baby spinach or arugula.

USE ALTERNATIVES

If you live in my area or somewhere with similar climate, the various ingredients in each salad should mostly be available locally around the same time, though beware, global warming is shifting things up! Get a jump-start on your creative process by utilizing the alternatives and substitutions suggested at the bottom of most of the recipes. Don't be afraid to substitute alternative veggies that are available in your area. After you build your muscle this way, launch your own creativity explosion by making up your own alternatives and substitutions.

CULTIVATE RADICAL EXPERIMENTATION

Use the recipes in this book as a starting point for more vegan adventures. Notice what tastes and taste combinations you like, and experiment with these. Use the techniques in the book with additional foods. For example if you liked the sweet potatoes in the Roasted Cardamom TriColor Sweet Potato Salad, try the same roasting technique with parsnips or rutabagas. If you like the dry sauté method used in the Spring Pasta Salad with Watercress and Shitake recipe, experiment with dry sautéing of other veggies. Or if you like the idea of reducing or eliminating extracted oils in your diet, use the technique I use in the dressing for the sweet potato salad just mentioned in other recipes.

CREATE NEW RECIPES

Use the Six Guiding Principles For Fabulous Flavor to create entirely new vegan recipes from scratch (and then share them with me; I would love to see what you create!).

The Recipes

About the Recipes

GENERAL INFORMATION ABOUT THE RECIPES

In this section are fifty recipes organized by type into seven chapters. Forty-one of the recipes are for salads; most of these recipes include dressings. There are also nine recipes for additional salad dressings. Each recipe includes an approximate yield, a list of ingredients, and directions in the form of listed steps. Most of the recipes also include a list of notes, substitutions, and variations. The ingredients for each recipe appear in the list in order of their use in the recipe. In some cases a single ingredient has more than one use within the recipe, for instance part of the ingredient may be used to braise another ingredient and part is used in the dressing. In these cases, the total amount needed for the recipes is included in the list of ingredients, followed by the word "divided." That way you will know not to use the full quantity the first time the ingredient is mentioned in the directions.

VEGETABLE QUANTITIES:

In many of these recipes I list ingredient quantities such as "2 medium carrots" or "½ large rutabaga." Vegetables vary tremendously in size! So do bunches of herbs and other ingredients used in these recipes. I have made an attempt to also include alternative ways of estimating amounts, for instance by saying "½ bunch cilantro (approximately ½ cup chopped)," but I have not done so for every recipe. I have included an approximate yield in every recipe, however. If the dish you make has a significantly different yield than what is listed, you may need to adjust the recipe in response. For example, if your yield is significantly smaller, you may need less salad dressing, and if larger, you may need more. Most of the recipes say "taste and adjust seasonings" toward the end. That is always an essential practice! The "seasonings" refers to whatever herbs, spices, garlic, chile peppers, oils, salt or salty substance, vinegars, and/or lemon or lime juice are included in the recipe.

ON WASHING AND TRIMMING VEGETABLES AND HERBS:

I strongly suggest washing all vegetables, fruits, and herbs before eating, with the exception of mushrooms, to remove soil, potential pathogens, and parasites. If you have purchased pre-washed greens, you can skip washing to save yourself time. Herbs and greens that have not been pre-washed benefit by a plunge in a large bowl of clear water, followed by a shake or spin in a salad spinner. A good stiff brush is handy for potatoes, carrots, rutabagas, beets, and other root crops.

TRIMMING IS ALSO ESSENTIAL.

Cut ends off of carrots, celery, cucumbers, summer squashes, eggplants, sweet potatoes, etc. Take the stem end off of snap peas and peel the strings out of the side seams of the pods. Remove stem ends from tomatoes. Remove eyes from potatoes. In the case of kale, collards, and similar greens, strip the leaves off of tough stems. Trim any tough stems from dill and cilantro, but use the majority of the stems since they are tender. Strip basil, mint, and watercress leaves from the stems. Give a similar treatment to perennial herbs such as rosemary, thyme, and sage. Mushrooms soak up water, so it is best to brush dirt off of them with a soft brush rather than washing. I leave stems on mushrooms, but might cut a bit off the end of the stem if it appears too dry or tough.

With few exceptions (such as winter squash), most vegetables do not require peeling, though peeling (or partial peeling) is a great idea for potatoes, beets, sweet potatoes, and other vegetables if they have lots of blemishes, scars, and hard spots on the skins. In general, trim off anything that doesn't appear appetizing. Discard if it is rotten, infested with insects, or oxidized. If the trimmings are merely cosmetically-challenged, it is fine to save for stock.

LEMONS AND LIMES:

In most of the recipes that call for lemons and limes I have given both an item quantity (e.g. 1–2 lemons) and a juice quantity (e.g. ¼ cup). These measurements should be taken as guidelines rather than absolutes. The reason for this is that citrus vary tremendously in size, juiciness, and tartness. A large, juicy Meyer lemon might have upwards of ¼ cup of sweet juice in it, whereas a similar sized Eureka might only yield 2 tablespoons. The juice from the Eureka will be more potent in its capacity to add zing to the food, however, as it is a very tart lemon compared to the Meyer. Please let your taste buds be the final authority of the amount of lemon and/or lime you use in the recipes.

WATER IN INGREDIENT LISTS:

Where a specific quantity of water is an ingredient in a recipe, for example in a salad dressing, a starting quantity of water is included in the ingredient list. Additional water may be needed for the desired consistency. Water used for cooking grains or legumes, or soaking things such as nuts and seaweeds is not included in the ingredients list.

GRAINS AND LEGUMES:

Several of the salads call for cooked grains and legumes. You might choose to cook them all yourself, or to use canned products in the case of legumes. Be sure to rinse dry beans and grains before cooking to remove dirt, dust, and other contaminants. If you are cooking the beans at home, be careful to prevent over-cooking as you don't want mashed beans in your salad! Tips that might help prevent the beans from splitting include soaking the beans, making sure you have ample water over the top of them while cooking, and cooking gently.

NUTS:

Chomping down on a hard nut shell is an unpleasant experience. I recommend you sort through nuts before chopping to look for bits of shell or other contaminants. Typically, I suggest coarsely chopping nuts for salad or leaving them whole, as tiny bits of nuts in a salad might give an unappealing texture and/or appearance. When coarsely chopping, some finer particles will collect on the cutting board. I advise leaving these out of the salad and just using the larger pieces. With walnuts and pecans, you might also consider simply breaking them up into halves or quarters.

CUTTING TERMS:

I use a number of terms to describe the cuts to make on the vegetables in the salad (and to some extent, the fruit). If you see "bite-sized pieces," I mean that one such piece is large enough to be a complete bite all by itself. Such a bite would be 1 inch or a little larger cubed. If the wording is "thinly slice," that means about ⅛ inch or thinner. Often I give a specific thickness, e.g. "¼ inch slices." Dicing is cutting into cubes or cube-like pieces. This is most easily accomplished by slicing the vegetable lengthwise, stacking the slices and cutting them into strips, then cutting across the strips. Mincing means to cut it up very small.

Green Salads

Playful Salad with Herbs and Flowers

Yield: 4–6 servings (about 8 cups)

INGREDIENTS:

4 ounces mixed baby greens such as arugula, claytonia, spinach, frisée, maché, sorrel, cress, fava bean leaves, baby kale, etc.

3 ounces large sprouts such as sunflower, buckwheat, or pea, or a mix of large sprouts

1 small carrot, grated

½ cup of mixed fresh herbs such as cilantro, parsley, basil, oregano, mint, thyme

½–1 cup edible flowers such as calendula, nasturtiums, marigolds, sage, lavender, borage, rosemary, alyssum, bachelor buttons, coriander, mustard, etc.

3 tablespoons raw shelled pine nuts

DIRECTIONS:

1. Place baby greens, sprouts, and grated carrots in salad bowl.
2. Strip leaves off of tough herb stems. Add leaves and tender tops of herbs to salad bowl.
3. Prep flowers for salad. Remove petals from large flowers like marigolds and calendula. Pull sage, lavender, borage, and rosemary flowers out of their calyces. Sprinkle some of the petals into the salad bowl and reserve some for garnish.
4. Toss salad to mix.
5. Garnish the salad with reserved flowers.
6. Sprinkle with pine nuts.
7. Serve with salad dressing of your choice.

NOTES, SUBSTITUTIONS, AND VARIATIONS:

Suggested dressings: Avocado Tahini Lime, Creamy Tarragon, Basic Balsamic, Creamy Dried Tomato and Basil, or Tahini Dill.

Use different nuts if you'd like. Or use sesame or pumpkin seeds.

Add additional seasonal veggies such as tomatoes, cucumbers, or radishes.

Avocados are another delightful addition.

The sprouts and flowers make this salad really playful. For a romantic experience, make one large plate of this salad and share it with your beloved, being sure to feed each other slowly and lovingly!

Celebration Kale Salad

Yield: 6 generous servings (about 8 cups)

INGREDIENTS:

1 bunch green kale (also called "curly kale")

1 medium red beet, grated

½ watermelon radish, cut vertically

½ small red onion, cut vertically, then thinly sliced horizontally

½ cup shredded unsweetened coconut, lightly packed

1 lemon, juiced to make about 2–3 tablespoons lemon juice, or more to taste

2 tablespoons garbanzo bean or other light miso

1 tablespoon extra-virgin olive oil

DIRECTIONS:

1. Strip kale leaves from stems. Reserve stems for another use (juicing, stock, etc.). Place leaves in a pile on a cutting board and cut across at one-inch intervals width-wise and lengthwise. Place in large bowl.
2. Add beets to kale in bowl.
3. Cut the watermelon radish half in half vertically again; then slice thinly across the quarters, making beautiful wedge-shaped slices. Add to veggies in bowl.
4. Separate the layers of the onion slices and add to bowl.
5. Add shredded coconut to bowl.
6. **Make dressing:**
   - In a small bowl, combine miso with the lemon juice, a little bit at a time, stirring to combine well.
   - When the mixture is a thick, but very moist paste, add remaining lemon juice and olive oil.
   - Mix well to combine.
7. Pour dressing over salad and mix everything together thoroughly. Taste. Make additional dressing if needed; add to salad and mix well.
8. Serve.

NOTES, SUBSTITUTIONS, AND VARIATIONS:

Two miso suggestions: South River Red Pepper and Garlic and Miso Master Organic Garbanzo Miso.

This salad can be made ahead and will stay good for a day or two, even dressed. Make extra dressing if you are making it ahead, as the veggies will soak up dressing overnight and it may taste better with additional dressing added before serving.

If watermelon radishes are not in season or available in your area, you can substitute 3–4 regular radishes or half of a rutabaga.

Baby Spinach with Spicy Braised Tempeh and Shiitake Sesame Dressing

Yield: 4–6 servings (about 8 cups)

INGREDIENTS:

1 eight-ounce package of tempeh

1 spicy fresh chile, stemmed and minced, optional

½ cup vegetable stock or water

2 tablespoons plus 1 teaspoon tamari, divided

½ teaspoon red pepper flakes

1 tablespoon prepared mustard

1 tablespoon apple cider vinegar

3 medium-sized shiitake mushrooms

2 tablespoons extra-virgin olive oil

2 tablespoons toasted sesame oil

½–1 lemon, juiced to make about 2 tablespoons lemon juice, or more to taste

2 cloves garlic, peeled and minced

Several sprigs cilantro, optional

2 tablespoons water, or more for consistency

6 ounces baby spinach

¼ medium red onion, thinly sliced

1 large avocado, pitted, peeled and cut into bite-sized pieces

DIRECTIONS:

1. Preheat oven to 350°.
2. Cut the tempeh into quarter-inch thick slices, then cross cut strips into squares. Spread tempeh pieces out in a baking pan.
3. Make braising liquid by combining chile, vegetable stock or water, 2 tablespoons tamari, red pepper flakes, prepared mustard, and apple cider vinegar.
4. Pour the braising liquid over the tempeh.
5. Place tempeh in the oven. Allow it to braise in the oven for about 15–20 minutes; then flip the pieces of tempeh over and return to the oven. Remove from oven when the liquid has all been absorbed and set aside to cool.
6. **Make dressing:**
    · Brush dirt off of mushrooms and remove ends of stems if funky.
    · Coarsely chop mushrooms.
    · Combine mushrooms, both oils, remaining teaspoon tamari, lemon juice, garlic, cilantro (if using), and water in a blender or food processor. Process until smooth.

- Add a little additional water if necessary to make a thick but pourable dressing.
7. **Assemble salad:**
    - Place the spinach on a serving platter or bowl.
    - Add the avocados, red onion, and cooled tempeh.
    - Pour the dressing over the salad and mix gently to combine. Or you can leave the dressing off and serve it at the table on the side.
8. Serve.

NOTES, SUBSTITUTIONS, AND VARIATIONS:

Reduce spiciness by removing seeds and white pith from chile.

Experiment with additional vegetables such as peas, lightly steamed asparagus, and/or tomatoes.

Reduce oil in the dressing by omitting the olive oil and instead using 1 teaspoon chia seeds soaked briefly in 2 tablespoons water.

You can make the dressing and tempeh ahead of time to be able to get the meal on the table quickly when it's time.

Baby Greens with Smoked Tofu and Kraut

Yield: 6–8 servings (about 8 cups)

INGREDIENTS:

4 ounces smoked tofu

¼ cup cilantro leaves and tender stems

1–2 lemons, juiced to make about ¼ cup lemon juice

3 tablespoons prepared mustard

3 tablespoons raw tahini

¼ cup water, or more for consistency

6–8 ounces baby salad greens

1 large tomato or 2–3 small ones, cut into bite-sized pieces

¼ medium red onion, thinly sliced

1 medium avocado, peeled, pitted, and cut into bite-sized pieces.

1 cup live fermented sauerkraut

Sprouts and edible flowers for garnish, optional

DIRECTIONS:

1. Slice smoked tofu. Cut slices into small pieces.
2. **Make dressing:**
   - Combine cilantro, lemon juice, mustard, tahini, and water in a blender or food processor. Process until smooth. Add a little additional water if necessary to make a pourable dressing.
3. Combine salad greens, tomatoes, onion, smoked tofu, avocado, and sauerkraut in a serving bowl. Pour dressing over salad and toss gently to combine.
4. Garnish with sprouts and flowers, if using.
5. Serve.

VARIATIONS AND SUBSTITUTIONS:

Experiment with additional vegetables such as cucumber, red or yellow bell pepper, and/or grated carrots.

Meal on the Table Now Variation: Make the dressing ahead of time for a relatively fast prep time.

Try using different flavored sauerkrauts.

Substitute another fresh herb for the cilantro. If you use a tender annual such as basil, dill, or parsley, maintain the same proportions. For perennials with more strongly flavored leaves such as oregano, thyme, and sage, you can use far less of the herb for a robust flavor.

Double Pea Salad with Roasted Potatoes

Yield: 4–6 servings (about 1½ –2 quarts)

INGREDIENTS:

4 small red potatoes (about 1 pound), cut into bite-sized pieces.

1–2 teaspoons melted coconut oil

Several pinches of sea salt, optional

½ fennel bulb, thinly sliced

½ pound snap peas, cut diagonally into ½-inch thick slices

4–6 ounces pea plant tops

DIRECTIONS:

1. Preheat oven to 450°.
2. Place potatoes on one or more baking pans. Don't overcrowd. Add melted coconut oil and salt, if using, and toss.
3. Put potatoes in the oven to roast, turning once or twice until tender and browned. This will take approximately 25–40 minutes.
4. Set potatoes aside to cool.
5. Remove leaves and tender tops of pea greens to use for salad, discarding tough stems or reserving them for another use.
6. Assemble salad by mounding the pea greens on a platter. Add cooled roasted potatoes and the other ingredients on top.
7. Serve with a creamy dressing or a vinaigrette.

NOTES, SUBSTITUTIONS, AND VARIATIONS:

Suggested dressings: Creamy Tarragon, Basic Balsamic, or Tahini Dill.

If you are avoiding oil, you can steam the potatoes. Or dry roast them:

- Preheat oven to 500°.
- Cut potatoes as instructed in the recipe.
- Place in an unoiled baking pan. A clay pan works great for dry roasting. Or use a cast iron pan if you have one. Be sure that your pieces of potato have the skin side down to reduce sticking.
- Place dish in the oven and roast for 40–50 minutes. They will get crunchy on the outside and nicely steamed inside.

If you are unable to find pea tops, substitute another tender mild-tasting green. If you have fava bean plants or miner's lettuce in your garden, leaves of these plants make excellent substitutes. Or you can use baby spinach or baby kale.

Another option is to use spicy greens such as arugula or cress, and pair with a strongly flavored and/or creamy dressing.

Meal on the Table Now Variation:
- When you are preparing roasted potatoes for another meal, prepare and roast an extra pound and set aside as leftovers.
- Use these leftovers within a day or so to make a super-speedy version of this salad.

Love House Salad

Yield: 6–8 servings (about 10 cups)

NOTE:

A "Love House Salad" is a standing feature at our house for lunch most days of the week. The exact composition of the salad varies with the seasons, though it typically contains a mixture of baby greens and fresh herbs from the garden, a generous pile of grated carrots, one or more avocados, and whatever other veggies we have on hand. Quite commonly, it also contains sprouts and edible flowers of various types.

The Love House Salad is made in layers and rarely tossed before serving. It is served without a dressing on it, and a variety of condiments are served on the side so each person can dress it up as she/he pleases. Sauerkraut, pumpkin seeds, hemp seeds, and hemp oil are very common toppings, and tahini dressing also makes an appearance on a semi-regular basis. This recipe documents a Love House Salad made in July 2016.

INGREDIENTS:

1 cup of leaves and tender stems of mixed fresh herbs such as cilantro, parsley, shiso, basil, oregano, mint, thyme

6 ounces mixed baby greens such as arugula, sorrel, cress, nasturtium leaves, baby bok choy, maché, baby kale, etc.

2 ounces mixed large sprouts such as sunflower, buckwheat, or pea, or a mix of large sprouts

2 carrots, grated

1 cucumber, sliced

1 red, orange, or yellow bell pepper, cut into strips

2 heirloom tomatoes, cut into bite-sized pieces

1 avocado, peeled, pitted, and cut into bite-sized pieces

3 tablespoons raw shelled pistachio nuts

2 tablespoons raw shelled pine nuts

1 cup edible flowers such as calendula, nasturtiums, marigolds, sage, lavender, borage, rosemary, allysum, bachelor's buttons, coriander, mustard, etc.

Side condiments to your taste, e.g. live sauerkraut, additional nuts and seeds, oil and vinegar, lemon wedges, salad dressing, etc.

DIRECTIONS:

1. Place baby greens and herbs in salad bowl, tossing to distribute herbs throughout.
2. Spread sprouts over the greens.
3. Add carrots, cucumber, bell pepper, tomatoes, and avocado to salad.
4. Sprinkle nuts over salad.
5. Prep flowers for salad. Remove petals from large flowers like marigolds and calendula. Pull sage, lavender, borage, and rosemary flowers out of their calyces. Leave nasturtiums and alyssum whole. Sprinkle the flowers over the salad.
6. Serve with condiments and/or salad dressing(s) of your choice.

Watercress Salad with Spring Veggies and Lemony Seed Dressing

Yield: 4–6 servings (about 8 cups)

INGREDIENTS:

2 tablespoons sunflower seeds
(note: these get soaked overnight)

2 tablespoons sesame seeds
(note: these get soaked overnight)

2 tablespoons pumpkin seeds
(note: these get soaked overnight)

6–8 spears asparagus

2 bunches watercress

4 ounces of snap peas, cut diagonally
into ½-inch pieces

½ large fennel bulb, halved lengthwise,
sliced crosswise

¼ cup fresh parsley leaves

1–1½ lemons, juiced to make about
3-4 tablespoons juice

¼ cup water, or more for consistency

1 large avocado, peeled, pitted,
quartered and sliced

6–8 nasturtium flowers, optional

DIRECTIONS:

1. Combine sunflower, sesame, and pumpkin seeds in a bowl. Cover with about 3 times their volume of water and leave to soak overnight. Drain and rinse before using.
2. Cut or snap off tough bottoms of stems of asparagus spears. Cut diagonally into ½-inch slices.
3. Place asparagus in steamer and steam over boiling water for 1–2 minutes until barely tender. Remove from pot and place in the fridge to cool.
4. Strip leaves and tender tops from watercress stems. Discard stems.
5. **Make dressing:**
   - In a blender or food processor, combine soaked seeds, parsley leaves, lemon juice, and water.
   - Blend until smooth, adding more water if needed to make it pourable.
   - Taste and adjust lemon juice.
6. Toss watercress leaves with snap peas, asparagus, and fennel.
7. Place avocado on salad.
8. Top with nasturtium blossoms, if using.
9. Serve with dressing on the side.

VARIATIONS AND SUBSTITUTIONS:

Try different edible flowers such as pansies, cornflowers, or calendula.

Substitute other spring vegetables for the asparagus, fennel, and peas, for example try cucumbers, radishes, and carrots.

Substitute a different dressing such as the Basic Balsamic Vinaigrette, Tahini Dill, or Oil-Free Chile Lime Poppy Seed Dressing.

Spinach Salad with Candied Pecans and Roasted Veggies Two Ways

Yield: 6–10 servings (about 2½ –3 quarts)

NOTE:

The roasted veggies for this salad can be prepared two ways. If you don't mind waiting and prefer less oil, use Version 1. If you want the veggies to be crusty and don't mind added oil, use Version 2, which is also the quicker method. Both methods result in deliciousness!

INGREDIENTS:

1 ½–2 pounds winter squash
(e.g. kabocha or buttercup)

1 pound beets

1 large yellow onion

1–2 tablespoons melted coconut oil, optional

Several pinches of sea salt, optional

¾ cup raw shelled pecan halves or pieces

¼ cup maple syrup

2–4 rosemary sprigs, enough to yield
1 scant tablespoon leaves

1½ tablespoons olive oil

3 tablespoons balsamic vinegar

1 large bunch spinach, cut into one-inch ribbons

DIRECTIONS:

1. Preheat oven to 450°.
2. **Prepare veggies, Version 1 (or skip to Version 2):**
   - Cut squash in half. Remove seeds. Place squash cut side down in a baking pan. Pierce several holes through the squash with a sharp knife.
   - Place whole beets in the baking pan with the squash.
   - Place whole onion in the baking pan with the squash and beet.
   - Cover pan with foil. Put in oven and dry roast until tender when poked with a fork but not falling apart. This will take approximately 55 minutes for the squash and up to 2 hours for the beets and onions, depending on their size.
   - Set veggies aside to cool. When cool enough to handle, peel onion and trim beet. Cut onion, squash, and beet into bite-sized pieces and allow them to cool completely.

3. **Prepare veggies, Version 2:**
   - Cut squash in half. Remove seeds. Peel and cut into fairly uniform bite-sized pieces.
   - Slice beets into quarters, then cross-slice quarters into slices about 1/2 inch thick.
   - Peel onion. Slice into thin wedges vertically.
   - Place veggies on separate baking pans. Don't overcrowd. Add melted coconut oil and salt (if using) to veggies and toss. Use about 1 teaspoon coconut oil and one small pinch of salt per pan. Put in oven and roast, turning and tossing occasionally until tender and browned. This will take approximately 25 minutes for the onions, 30 minutes for the beets, and 40 minutes for the squash.
   - Set veggies aside to cool.

4. **Prepare candied pecans:**
   - Grease a plate with a small amount of coconut oil.
   - Sort through pecans to remove shells and bad nuts.
   - Cook maple syrup in a small pan, stirring regularly, until it reaches hard ball stage. This stage is reached when a small bit of syrup is dropped into a cup of cold water and it turns hard. Remove from heat.
   - Add pecans to syrup, stirring to coat nuts.
   - Quickly spread pecans on the greased plate to cool, using one or two forks to separate clumps as well as possible.
5. **Make dressing:**
   - Remove rosemary leaves from stems. Discard stems or reserve for another use. Mince leaves.
   - Mix rosemary, olive oil, and vinegar together in a small jar with a fitted lid. Cover jar and shake to combine.
6. When roasted veggies are cool, combine with spinach and nuts. Mix gently.
7. Add vinaigrette to taste and serve immediately.

Chopped & Shredded Salads

Cucumber Dill Raita Salad

Yield: 6 servings (about 5–6 cups)

INGREDIENTS:

4 cucumbers, diced into ¼-inch pieces

½ cup raw walnut halves or pieces, coarsely chopped

1 clove garlic, peeled and minced

¼ teaspoon sea salt

½ large bunch of fresh dill (enough to yield approximately ⅝ cup chopped)

1 cup plain, unsweetened coconut yogurt

Part of a lemon, juiced to make about 1 teaspoon lemon juice, optional

DIRECTIONS:

1. Combine cucumbers, walnuts, and garlic in a bowl with salt; set aside.
2. Remove tough parts of dill stems. Coarsely chop leaves and tender stems.
3. Add dill and coconut yogurt to cucumber mixture. Mix thoroughly.
4. Taste salad. If your coconut yogurt is not very tart, you may want to add a little lemon juice to increase the tartness.
5. Serve.

NOTES, SUBSTITUTIONS, AND VARIATIONS:

You can get a delightful, slightly pickled effect by leaving the salted cucumbers and walnuts in a bowl in the refrigerator for several hours or overnight. Use ½ teaspoon of salt if you are pickling the cucumbers. When ready to complete the salad, drain most of the liquid off (which will reduce the salt content); then proceed as above.

Using mint instead of dill makes for a wonderful variation.

You can substitute plain, unsweetened soy yogurt for the coconut yogurt.

Omit walnuts if you'd like, or substitute pecans.

If you are handy with fresh young coconuts, you can make a delightful homemade coconut yogurt by blending the flesh of young coconuts with enough water to make a smooth, thick cream. Place the coconut cream in a jar or glass or ceramic bowl. Stir in the contents of one probiotic supplement capsule. Leave to culture in a warm place for 8–12 hours or until it is tart enough for your taste. Yum!

Napa Cabbage and Hijiki Salad with Toasted Sesame Dressing

Yield: 6 servings (about 5–7 cups)

INGREDIENTS:

2 tablespoons dry hijiki seaweed

1 small head Napa cabbage
(about 4 cups shredded)

1 carrot, grated

5–8 radishes, thinly sliced

¼ cup brown or black sesame seeds

2 tablespoons toasted sesame oil

3 tablespoons brown rice vinegar

1 tablespoon tamari

2 teaspoons grated fresh ginger root

½ teaspoon red pepper flakes, or more to taste

Half a bunch of cilantro, coarsely chopped (about 1 cup chopped)

DIRECTIONS:

1. Put hijiki in a bowl and cover with about 1 cup of water. Allow to soak for at least 20 minutes, preferably longer.
2. Remove leaves of Napa cabbage from core and trim off the bottom end. Slice horizontally into thin strips, cutting across both the leafy part and the center rib.
3. **Make dressing:**
   · Mix sesame oil, vinegar, tamari, grated ginger, and red pepper flakes in a small jar with a fitted lid.
   · Cover jar and shake to combine.
4. Drain hijiki. Discard liquid.
5. Combine Napa cabbage, hijiki, carrot, radish, sesame seeds, cilantro, and dressing in salad bowl.
6. Mix well to combine. Taste and adjust seasonings.
7. Serve.

NOTES, SUBSTITUTIONS, AND VARIATIONS:

Make this salad into a quick one-course meal by doubling ingredient quantities, soaking the hijiki in advance, and adding thin strips of smoked tofu and pine nuts or chopped almonds. Or leave out the tofu or nuts and serve with brown rice cakes with tahini spread on them.

Add other veggies in season, such as sliced red or yellow bell peppers, thinly sliced daikon radish, sliced sugar snap peas, or sliced cucumber.

Add shelled edamame.

Try substituting Vietnamese coriander or shiso leaves for the cilantro.

Minted Lemon Spice Salad

Yield: 4–6 servings (about 5–6 cups)

INGREDIENTS:

2 medium zucchinis, diced into ¼-inch pieces

3 small carrots, halved or quartered lengthwise then thinly sliced

3 stalks celery, thinly sliced

1 large watermelon radish, diced into ¼-inch pieces

1–3 moderately spicy chiles such as jalapeños, rocotos, or serranos, to taste

¼ cup raw shelled macadamia nuts or Brazil nuts, coarsely chopped

1–2 lemons, juiced as directed in recipe, or more to taste

1 bunch of fresh mint

1 teaspoon umeboshi vinegar

DIRECTIONS:

1. Quarter chile(s). Remove seeds and pith. Slice very thinly across the quarters.
2. Mix all veggies together in a salad bowl.
3. Add chopped nuts to salad.
4. Juice first lemon.
5. Remove mint leaves from tough stems. Discard stems or save for another use. Mince leaves.
6. Add lemon juice, umeboshi vinegar, and mint to salad and mix well.
7. Taste salad. If needed, juice the second lemon and add more to taste.

NOTES, VARIATIONS, SUBSTITUTIONS:

If you don't have umeboshi vinegar, substitute a small pinch of sea salt and additional lemon juice to taste.

If you can't find watermelon radish, I'm so sorry to hear that! It lends such a lovely color to the salad. One substitute that would provide some pink color and some brassica taste is one half of a candy-striped beet and one half of a rutabaga. Or substitute another root veggie such as celery root, sunchoke, or turnip.

This salad keeps well for a few days in the fridge.

Corn Salad with Chipotle and Lime

Yield: 8–10 servings (about 10–12 cups)

INGREDIENTS:

1–2 dried chipotle peppers

6–7 ears of corn

2 large red bell peppers, cut into 1 inch matchsticks

1 pound zucchini, diced into ¼-inch pieces

½ cup sliced Kalamata olives

½ cup raw shelled macadamia nuts or filberts, coarsely chopped

½ bunch cilantro

2–3 limes, juiced to make about ¼ cup lime juice, or more to taste

1 teaspoon umeboshi paste, optional, or more to taste

DIRECTIONS:

1. Slice chipotle(s) open and soak in a cup or very small bowl in hot water to cover.
2. Shuck and de-silk corn; cut kernels off the cobs.
3. Coarsely chop cilantro including all of the tender stems.
4. Drain chipotle, reserving liquid.
5. Remove stems from chipotle. Chop fairly fine.
6. Mix umeboshi paste with some of the lime juice to make it distribute more easily.
7. Combine all ingredients, including reserved chipotle soaking liquid, and mix well.
8. Taste and adjust seasonings (umeboshi, lime, chipotle, cilantro).

NOTES, SUBSTITUTIONS, AND VARIATIONS:

If you do not have umeboshi paste, you can substitute additional lime juice and a little sea salt.

You can substitute other varieties of olive or nuts.

Possible veggies to add include tomatoes, cucumber, and snap beans.

The addition of unsalted dried tomatoes is also quite lovely.

This salad works very well as trail food. Add additional lime juice. Spread on dehydrator sheets and dehydrate at 115° Fahrenheit. When moisture content is minimal, pack for the trail. Each cup of fresh salad makes about ⅜ cup dried, which will make approximately ½ cup reconstituted.

Winter Root Slaw with Coconut Yogurt & Dill

Yield: 6–10 servings (about 4–5 cups)

INGREDIENTS:

½ medium rutabaga (about ½ pound)

1 large watermelon radish (about ½ pound), or use substitute as described below

2 medium carrots (about ½ pound)

1 medium yellow beet (about ½ pound)

1 medium red beet (about ½ pound)

1 bunch fresh dill

1 cup plain unsweetened coconut yogurt

2 tablespoons water, or more for consistency

½ lemon, juiced to make about 1–2 teaspoons lemon juice, optional

DIRECTIONS:

1. Grate each vegetable in turn, placing the shreds of each in a separate container.

2. If you do not have watermelon radish, double the rutabaga quantity. After grating the red beets, lightly stain half of the rutabaga with beet juice by squeezing some grated beets over the rutabaga and mixing the dye throughout. You should have lovely pink rutabaga shreds.

3. **Make dressing:**
   · Cut or break off coarse stems of the dill. Discard stems.
   · Combine dill, coconut yogurt, and water in a blender or food processor and process until smooth.

- Taste. Add lemon juice if you want more tang. Add additional water if it needs to be thinner.
4. Arrange grated veggies on a platter in a design of your choice.
5. Serve with the dressing on the side.

NOTES, SUBSTITUTIONS, AND VARIATIONS:

The order of appearance in the ingredient list is the suggested grating order if you don't want to thoroughly clean your grater between veggies, as that order will minimize cross-contamination of colors. A grating blade on a food processor works well if you have one.

You can also mix all the grated root veggies together in a serving bowl, add the dressing and thoroughly combine, and serve it that way. The dressing will tone down the vivid colors of the veggies, and the red beet will tend to stain everything, but it will still be delicious!

You can substitute plain unsweetened soy yogurt for the coconut yogurt.

Substitute a different fresh herb such as parsley or mint for the dill.

Substitute a different dressing. Other dressings that work well with the root slaw are Tahini Dill, Creamy Tarragon, and Avocado Tahini Lime.

Asian Fusion Hijiki Salad

Yield: 6–12 servings (about 6–8 cups)

INGREDIENTS:

1 cup shelled edamame

½ ounce dry hijiki seaweed

½ large cucumber, cut into 1½-inch long matchsticks

2 medium carrots, grated

1–2 celery stalks, cut into ¼-inch slices (enough for ½ cup)

Cauliflower, cut into small florets (enough for ½ cup florets)

2 ounces smoked tofu, cut into 1½-inch long matchsticks

2 tablespoons raw shelled pine nuts

1 red or yellow bell pepper (or half of each), cut into 1½-inch long matchsticks

1 or 2 green onions, thinly sliced (use both green and white parts)

½ bunch cilantro

2 rounded tablespoons grated fresh ginger

2 cloves garlic, peeled and minced

1½ tablespoons brown rice vinegar, or more to taste

1½ tablespoon tamari, or more to taste

2 tablespoons toasted sesame oil, or more to taste

1 teaspoon red pepper flakes

½ teaspoon umeboshi vinegar or 1 teaspoon umeboshi paste

½ cup sesame seeds

DIRECTIONS:

1. If edamame is frozen, remove from freezer and measure out 1 cup. Leave it at room temperature to thaw while you prepare other ingredients.
2. Soak hijiki in a large bowl with several times its volume of water. Soak for an hour or longer.
3. Remove tough bottom stems of cilantro, then roughly chop the leaves and tender stems.
4. **Make dressing:**
   - Mix ginger, garlic, brown rice vinegar, tamari, toasted sesame oil, red pepper flakes, and umeboshi (vinegar or paste), in a small jar with a fitted lid.
   - Cover jar and shake to combine.
5. When hijiki has soaked for an hour or more and has at least doubled in volume, drain well, discarding liquid.
6. Combine hijiki with prepared veggies, tofu, cilantro, salad dressing, and sesame seeds.
7. Mix well and taste to adjust seasonings (tamari, toasted sesame oil, rice vinegar, red pepper flakes, ginger, garlic, umeboshi). Serve.

NOTES, VARIATIONS, AND SUBSTITUTIONS:

Shelled edamame is often available in the frozen vegetable section of your local grocery store.

If hijiki seaweed is not available, you can substitute arame seaweed.

This salad will keep well for several days in the refrigerator.

Try different nuts instead of pine nuts, for example macadamia nuts or almonds.

Use different seasonal vegetables. Others that work well in this dish include snap peas, green beans, radishes, and fennel.

Substitute strips of cooked tempeh for the smoked tofu.

Add more red pepper flakes or a chopped fresh ripe chile if you want more heat.

If you avoid soy in your diet, omit the smoked tofu. Substitute 1½ additional teaspoons umeboshi paste or 2 teaspoons additional umeboshi vinegar for the tamari, then adjust to taste. Substitute frozen or fresh shelled peas for edamame.

Other Land & Sea Vegetable Salads

Simple Cucumber Salad with Lemon Thyme and Chives

Yield: 4–6 servings (about 4–5 cups)

INGREDIENTS:

3 medium cucumbers, thinly sliced

1 tablespoon lemon thyme leaves, minced

2 tablespoons fresh chives, minced

½–1 lemon, juiced to make about 2 tablespoons fresh lemon juice

Pinch of sea salt, optional

DIRECTIONS:

1. Cut off stem ends of cucumbers. Thinly slice with a knife or mandoline, and put the sliced cucumbers in a serving bowl.
2. **Make dressing:**
   - Mix lemon juice, thyme, chives, and salt in a small jar with a fitted lid.
   - Cover jar and shake to combine.
3. Pour dressing over cucumbers. Toss to combine.
4. Taste salad and adjust seasonings.
5. Serve

VARIATIONS AND SUBSTITUTIONS:

Experiment with different herbs in the dressing, e.g. sage, oregano, rosemary, basil, different types of thyme, etc.

Use specialty cucumbers such as lemon cucumbers or Armenian cucumbers.

Add freshly ground black pepper.

Heirloom Tomato and Avocado Salad with Basil and Lime

Yield: 4–6 servings (about 4–5 cups)

INGREDIENTS:

2 large heirloom tomatoes, sliced into thin wedges

1 large or 2 small avocados, quartered, peeled, pitted, and sliced vertically

1–2 cloves garlic, peeled and minced

1 tablespoon extra-virgin olive oil

2 tablespoons fresh lime juice

¼–½ cup fresh basil leaves, cut into thin ribbons

DIRECTIONS:

1. **Make dressing:**
   - Mix garlic, lime juice, and olive oil in a small jar with a fitted lid.
   - Cover jar and shake to combine.
2. Put tomatoes and avocados in a serving bowl or tray.
3. Scatter the basil ribbons over the tomatoes and avocados.
4. Pour dressing over salad and toss gently to distribute.
5. Serve.

VARIATIONS AND SUBSTITUTIONS:

Try using a combination of colors of heirloom tomatoes.

Substitute another fresh herb for the basil. Other herbs that would work well are mint, dill, and cilantro.

Use lemon juice or red wine vinegar instead of lime juice.

Sprinkle pine nuts or chopped pecans on top.

Sea Palm Frond Salad

Yield: 4–6 servings (about 5–6 cups)

INGREDIENTS:

1 ounce dried sea palm fronds (note: this gets soaked overnight, if possible)

1 cucumber, quartered lengthwise, then thinly sliced

1 red, orange, or yellow bell pepper, cut into thin strips

2 cups celery, thinly sliced

½ bunch cilantro (about 1 cup lightly packed)

2 green onions, thinly sliced (use both green and white parts)

2–4 cloves garlic, peeled and minced

1 tablespoon finely grated fresh ginger

1–2 lemons, juiced to make about ¼ cup lemon juice

2 tablespoons extra-virgin olive oil

1 tablespoon toasted sesame oil

2 teaspoons tamari

DIRECTIONS:

1. Soak the sea palm fronds in 3–4 cups of water for several hours or preferably overnight.

2. Remove tough bottom end of cilantro stems. Coarsely chop leaves and tender stems.

3. **Make dressing:**
   - Combine garlic, ginger, lemon juice, olive oil, toasted sesame oil, and tamari in a small jar with a fitted lid.
   - Cover jar and shake to combine.

4. Test the sea palm fronds. If they are not tender enough for your taste, cook them for about 5–15 minutes, checking occasionally. Avoid overcooking fronds to the point of falling apart. When tender enough, drain and cool.

5. In a bowl, combine sea palm fronds, cucumber, bell pepper, celery, cilantro, and green onions.

6. Pour dressing over salad. Toss. Taste and adjust seasonings and toss again.

7. Serve.

NOTES, SUBSTITUTIONS, AND VARIATIONS:

Substitute another fresh herb for the cilantro. Other herbs that would work well are parsley, Vietnamese coriander, mint, chives, and shiso.

Add red pepper flakes or a fresh minced chiles if you want it spicier.

Substitute seasonal vegetables when peppers are not in season. For instance, try grated carrots or thinly sliced radishes.

Marinated Veggie Medley on Mixed Greens

Yield: 4–8 servings (about 8–9 cups, plus greens)

INGREDIENTS:

1½ cups cooked or 1 15-ounce can garbanzo beans, drained and rinsed

2 medium carrots, thinly sliced

1 cucumber, thinly sliced

Cauliflower, cut into small florets (enough for 1 cup florets)

8 ounces Crimini mushrooms, thickly sliced

2 shallots, thinly sliced (about ¼–½ cup)

1 bunch cilantro

2 tablespoons fresh oregano leaves

2–4 cloves garlic, peeled and minced

2–4 lemons, juiced to make about ½ cup plus 1 tablespoon lemon juice, or more to taste

2 tablespoons red wine vinegar

¼ cup extra-virgin olive oil

1 teaspoon red pepper flakes

½ teaspoon black pepper

⅛ teaspoon sea salt

6–8 ounces mixed baby greens (or sprouts if layering in jars)

DIRECTIONS:

1. Remove bottom parts of cilantro stems, if tough. Coarsely chop.
2. Combine prepared vegetables, beans, and cilantro in a bowl.
3. **Make dressing:**
   - Strip oregano leaves and tops from tough stems. Mince.
   - Combine oregano, garlic, lemon juice, red wine vinegar, olive oil, red pepper flakes, black pepper, and sea salt in a small jar with a fitted lid.
   - Cover jar and shake to combine.
4. Pour salad dressing over salad. Mix gently to thoroughly combine.
5. Taste and adjust seasonings.
6. Refrigerate for 2 hours or up to overnight to allow veggies to marinate. Taste and adjust seasonings again.
7. Serve on a bed of mixed baby greens.

NOTE, VARIATIONS, AND SUBSTITUTIONS:

The marinated veggies, minus baby greens, keep well for several days in the fridge.

Use different seasonal vegetables. Others that work well in this dish include snap peas, green beans, zucchini or other summer squash, red or yellow peppers, corn, and tomatoes.

Experiment with different beans. Use another variety of beans such as red kidney or black beans.

Add more red pepper flakes or a chopped fresh ripe hot pepper if you want more heat.

Experiment with different herbs.

This makes a great layered salad in a jar. Using four pint jars, divide ingredients evenly between the jars in layers. These can keep, covered, in the refrigerator for several days and be easily taken to work for lunch or out to picnics. To make the jar version, prepare all ingredients but do not combine them. Make your dressing. In a bowl, combine the drained and rinsed beans with 2 tablespoons of dressing, the shallots, and the cilantro. In a separate bowl, combine mushrooms with 3 tablespoons of dressing. Leave these two bowls of food to marinate a little, stirring occasionally, while you assemble the jars. Layer ingredients, distributing each ingredient equally between the four jars. Suggested order from bottom: cauliflower, carrots, bean mixture, cucumber, mushrooms, remaining dressing, sprouts.

Creamy Dill Potato Kraut Salad

Yield: 6–8 servings (about 2½ quarts)

INGREDIENTS:

1 cup "raw" (untoasted, unsalted) cashews (note: these get soaked overnight)

4 medium red potatoes, quartered

1 cucumber, thinly sliced

Several celery stalks with leaves, thinly sliced, enough for about 1 cup when sliced

1 small red onion, thinly sliced

1 small bunch fresh dill

1½ cups live fermented undrained sauerkraut, divided, or more to taste

½ teaspoon umeboshi vinegar, or to taste

½ cup water, or more for consistency

½ pound baby spinach or other baby greens

1 large or 2 small avocados

⅜ cup raw shelled pine nuts

DIRECTIONS:

1. Soak cashews in double or triple their volume of water for 6–24 hours.
2. Place potatoes in steamer and steam over boiling water, covered. Maintain a light boil until the potatoes are tender, but not overcooked, about 15–20 minutes. When done, remove from heat and leave uncovered to cool.
3. While potatoes are steaming, prep the other veggies.
4. Cut or tear off the tough bottom parts of the dill stems. Set aside half of the bunch of dill, and chop the other half crosswise at about ¼-inch intervals.
5. When the potatoes are done and cool enough to handle, cut each quarter potato into bite-sized pieces and put them in a mixing bowl.
6. Drain 1–2 tablespoons of the brine (liquid) from the sauerkraut over the potatoes and mix gently. Put marinating potatoes in the refrigerator to finish cooling.
7. **Make dressing:**
   - In a blender or food processor, combine soaked, drained, and rinsed cashews with remaining (uncut) dill, 1 cup sauerkraut including some brine, ½ teaspoon umeboshi vinegar, and water.
   - Process until smooth.
   - Add more water if needed to form a smooth, thick, and pourable dressing.

8. When potatoes are cool, remove from fridge and add cucumbers, celery, red onions, remaining sauerkraut, and brine, chopped fresh dill, and dressing. Mix gently but thoroughly to combine all ingredients.

9. **To serve:**
   - Place the spinach on individual plates or an attractive serving platter.
   - Mound the potato salad on the spinach, leaving a ring of spinach showing around the edges.
   - Slice avocado and attractively arrange on top of the individual plates or serving platter.
   - Sprinkle with pine nuts and serve.

NOTES, SUBSTITUTIONS, AND VARIATIONS:

If you are unable to soak the cashews, use about 1½ cups of unsoaked cashews and add additional water to process.

This recipe uses live, fermented sauerkraut. If you have it in your local markets it would be in a refrigerated section. Suggested varieties to complement this dish include garlic and dill flavored, plain, or with caraway seeds.

If live sauerkraut is unavailable in your area, pasteurized sauerkraut in a jar can be substituted. Determine quantity based on taste, as these krauts would most likely be much saltier than the live variety.

If umeboshi vinegar is unavailable in your area, you can substitute salt and / or extra sauerkraut to taste.

If you have allergies to nuts, substitute pumpkin seeds for the cashews and sesame seeds or sunflower seeds for the pine nuts.

It is fine to substitute other varieties of potatoes for the red potatoes. If using a potato with rough skin, such as a russet, you may choose to peel the potato for aesthetic and flavor reasons.

Use cilantro instead of dill and live fermented vegan kimchee instead of the sauerkraut.

Use basil instead of dill and use plain sauerkraut or a kraut flavor you can obtain locally that complements basil.

Use alternative nuts instead of pine nuts.

Add raw garlic to the salad dressing, especially if the kraut you are using does not have garlic in it.

Indian Spiced Beet and Coconut Salad

Yield: 6–8 servings (about 6–7 cups)

INGREDIENTS:

4–6 beets (enough for about 4 cups cubed), cut into bite-sized cubes.

1 teaspoon coriander seed

2 teaspoons decorticated cardamom seeds

1 teaspoon black seeds (perilla)

1 teaspoon brown or yellow mustard seeds

2 teaspoons cumin seeds

2 teaspoons fennel seeds

2 teaspoons fresh grated turmeric root (or substitute ½ teaspoon turmeric powder)

1 cup canned coconut milk, divided

½ cup vegetable stock, or more if needed

1 tablespoon coconut sugar, optional

1–2 limes, juiced to make about 3 tablespoons lime juice, divided

½ cup cilantro leaves and tender stems

¼ cup shredded unsweetened coconut

4–6 ounces spinach, full grown or baby

DIRECTIONS:

1. Coarsely grind the coriander and cardamom seeds in a spice grinder or with a mortar and pestle.
2. Mix all the spices except the turmeric together.
3. Pour ¾ cup of the coconut milk into a saucepan that is big enough to fit the beet pieces in one layer.
4. Heat the coconut milk to a boil; then add the spices. Continue cooking at a low boil, stirring occasionally, until the spices are fragrant.
5. Add the fresh or dry turmeric and cook a little longer, stirring.
6. Add the vegetable stock and coconut sugar (if using) to the pan and mix to combine with the spiced coconut milk.
7. Add the beets. Stir to coat the beets with the liquid. Turn the heat up to high to return the pan to a boil; then turn down to a simmer and cover.
8. Remove tough stems of cilantro and coarsely chop.
9. Keep the beets simmering until they are barely tender, stirring occasionally. Add additional stock if necessary to keep them from sticking.
10. When the beets are almost done, remove the cover. Turn up the heat and cook, stirring constantly, until the liquid has all evaporated off. Remove from heat and add 1 tablespoon lime juice, stirring to combine well. Allow beets to cool.
11. **Make dressing:**
    - Scrape the spicy beet-colored goo out of the pan you used to cook the beets.
    - If your remaining ¼ cup coconut milk is cold and super thick, mix it to liquefy it, or use a little heat if necessary.
    - Mix liquefied coconut milk, scrapings from beet pan, and remaining 2 tablespoons lime juice in a small jar with a fitted lid. Cover jar and shake to combine.
12. When beets are cool, add the shredded coconut and cilantro, and mix together.
13. Cut the spinach leaves into wide ribbons, if using fully grown spinach. Skip this step if using pre-washed baby greens.
14. Make a nest of spinach on a serving platter or bowl.
15. Mound the beets on the spinach.
16. Serve with the dressing on the side.

NOTES, VARIATIONS, AND SUBSTITUTIONS:

You can use any color beets for this salad. If you want to use a combination of golden and red beets, try making them in two separate pans, dividing the ingredients equally between them. This will ensure that the golden beets are still golden after cooking, instead of being dyed by the red ones.

You can use different greens for the nest.

If you want the beets spicy, add a couple of tablespoons of grated ginger and a pinch of cayenne to the spices you cook in the coconut milk.

Try using a combination of beets and another root veggie such as carrots or parsnips. Again, if using red beets, you may want to cook them separately from the lighter-colored veggies.

Use mint, basil, or Thai basil instead of cilantro.

If you don't have vegetable stock, replace it with water or additional coconut milk.

Cardamom Roasted TriColor Sweet Potatoes with Dried Cranberries and Pecans

Yield: 4–6 servings (about 6 cups)

INGREDIENTS:

1 pound assorted sweet potatoes and yams, in three colors if available, cut into bite-sized pieces

2 teaspoons virgin coconut oil

Pinch of sea salt

1 teaspoon decorticated cardamom seeds

¾ cup pomegranate juice

2 tablespoons chia seeds

4 ounces baby arugula

½ cup raw shelled pecan halves or pieces

¼ cup juice-sweetened dried cranberries

Fresh lemon juice to taste, optional

DIRECTIONS:

1. Preheat oven to 450°.
2. Spread sweet potato pieces out in a baking pan that is large enough for them to be in a single layer with space between them, so they will roast rather than steam.
3. Put the coconut oil in the pan with the potatoes, and place the pan in the oven for a minute or two to melt the oil.
4. Coarsely grind the cardamom seeds in a seed, spice, or coffee grinder.
5. Remove pan from oven. Sprinkle with salt and cardamom. Using a spatula, turn and mix sweet potatoes until they are coated with oil, and the salt, cardamom, and oil are evenly distributed throughout.
6. Spread sweet potatoes out with space between them, then place back in the oven when the oven is fully pre-heated.
7. Roast for about 20–25 minutes or until browning has begun. Remove from oven and turn them over with a spatula. Return to oven for another 10–15 more minutes, or long enough to be browned and crunchy on the outside.
8. While the sweet potatoes are roasting, make salad dressing by stirring chia seeds into pomegranate juice and leave to gel, stirring occasionally.
9. When sweet potatoes are done, remove from the oven and set aside to cool.

10. **To serve:**
    - Place the arugula in a salad bowl or platter.
    - Scatter the cooled sweet potatoes on top of the arugula, then scatter the pecans and cranberries on the salad.
    - Taste the salad dressing. Add lemon juice if you want it a little more tartly flavored.
    - If serving right away, you can pour the dressing over the salad and toss. Or leave the dressing off and let people add it to their servings at the table.

NOTES, SUBSTITUTIONS, AND VARIATIONS:

Regarding the colors of sweet potatoes: Hana and Japanese sweet potatoes are off-white to cream-colored inside. Garnet and Jewel yams are various shades of orange. Several varieties of purple sweet potatoes are available in some times and places. If three colors of sweet potatoes and yams are not available, just use what you can find. It will still be beautiful and delicious!

The dressing for this salad is oil-free. Whole chia seeds are used to provide the mouth-feel and stickiness of oil in a dressing. This technique can be used in other dressings for those wishing to reduce or avoid extracted oils.

The arugula is wonderful for this salad because its mild spiciness nicely offsets the sweet and fruity flavors of the sweet potatoes, cranberries, and fruit juice dressing. If you do not like spicy greens however, or if arugula is unavailable, you can substitute any baby greens, large sprouts, and/or romaine lettuce.

If you cannot find pomegranate juice you can use unsweetened cranberry juice. The chia seeds will not thicken the juice as well due to its high acid content, so make a gel first of the chia seeds in 3 tablespoons of water. Then add ½ cup of unsweetened cranberry juice. Taste, and add a very small amount of agave nectar or maple syrup if it is too tart for you. Don't make it too sweet, or it won't provide a contrast for the sweet potatoes.

Use dried cherries and unsweetened tart cherry juice instead of the cranberries and pomegranate juice.

Substitute 1½ teaspoons of five-spice powder for the cardamom. You can purchase pre-made five-spice powder, or make your own by combining star anise, cinnamon, fennel seeds, Sichuan pepper, and cloves in a spice grinder and grinding to a fine powder.

Meal on the Table Now Variation:
- Double the quantity of sweet potatoes, coconut oil, salt, and cardamom.
- Make the roasted sweet potatoes for a meal when you have more time for food prep. Eat half of the sweet potatoes as a side veggie for that meal, and put the other half in the fridge for your Meal on the Table Now meal.
- On the day of the Meal on the Table Now meal, begin by making the dressing. While the dressing gels, throw your arugula, reserved sweet potatoes, pecans, and dried cranberries in a salad bowl.
- Dress and serve with a simple side such as crackers and nut butter. Voila! Lunch or dinner in less than 10 minutes.

South of the Border Potato Salad with Pumpkin Seed Chipotle Dressing

Yield: 6–8 servings (about 6–7 cups)

INGREDIENTS:

½ cup pumpkin seeds
(note: these get soaked overnight)

2 pounds red potatoes or other thin-skinned variety (about 4–5 medium potatoes), cut into quarters

2 cobs corn, or 1½ cups frozen corn

4–5 small tomatoes, diced into large pieces (about 2 cups chopped)

½ cup cilantro leaves and tender stems

2–4 dried chipotle peppers

1–2 limes, juiced to make about ¼ cup lime juice

¼–½ teaspoon sea salt

¼ cup water, or more for consistency

DIRECTIONS:

1. Soak the pumpkin seeds in double or triple their volume of water overnight.
2. Place potatoes in steamer and steam over boiling water, covered. Maintain a light boil until the potatoes are tender, but not overcooked, about 15–20 minutes. When done, remove from heat and leave uncovered to cool.
3. Cut chipotles in half. If you want a really mild dressing, remove most or all of the seeds. Put chipotles (with or without seeds) in a cup or small bowl. Cover with water and leave to soak.
4. If using fresh corn, shuck and de-silk corn; cut kernels off the cobs.
5. Coarsely chop cilantro leaves and tender stems.
6. **Make dressing:**
   - Remove chipotles from soaking liquid and reserve the liquid.
   - In a blender or food processor, combine soaked pumpkin seeds, chipotles, lime juice, 2 tablespoons of the chipotle soaking water, salt, and water.
   - Process until smooth, adding more water or chipotle soaking water if needed.
   - Taste and adjust seasonings.
7. When potatoes have cooled, cut into large bite-sized pieces.
8. Combine potatoes with corn, tomatoes, cilantro, and salad dressing. Mix gently but thoroughly to combine.
9. Taste salad and adjust seasonings.
10. Place on a serving platter or serving bowl and garnish if you like.
11. Serve.

NOTES, SUBSTITUTIONS, AND VARIATIONS:

Add additional veggies such as cucumber, red or yellow bell pepper, or thinly sliced zucchini.

Serve on a bed of salad greens.

Substitute almonds or sunflower seeds for the pumpkin seeds.

Increase the smoky flavor by substituting smoked sea salt for the regular sea salt, or by adding smoked paprika or chipotle powder.

Grain & Legume Salads

Mixed Bean Salad with Tarragon & Lemon

Yield: 6–8 servings (about 7–8 cups without greens)

INGREDIENTS:

1 cup shelled edamame

4½ cups cooked or 3 15-ounce cans assorted beans (such as navy, black, small red, garbanzo, etc.), drained and rinsed

1 medium cucumber, cut into quarters lengthwise, then into ¼-inch slices crosswise

2 small carrots, thinly sliced (enough for 1 cup sliced)

Several stalks of celery, thinly sliced (enough for 1 cup sliced)

¼ small red onion, thinly sliced

2–4 lemons, juiced to make about ½ cup lemon juice, or more to taste

1 small bunch fresh tarragon (enough for about ¼ cup minced)

2–4 cloves garlic, peeled and minced

½ teaspoon umeboshi plum paste

2 tablespoons extra-virgin olive oil

Pinch of sea salt

4–6 ounces baby salad greens or large sprouts such as sunflower, buckwheat, or pea

DIRECTIONS:

1. If edamame is frozen, remove from freezer and measure out 1 cup. Leave it at room temperature to thaw while you prepare other ingredients.
2. Combine beans and prepared vegetables in a mixing bowl.
3. **Make dressing:**
   - Strip tarragon leaves and tender tops from tough stems. Mince.
   - Mix some of the lemon juice with the umeboshi paste in a small jar with a fitted lid. Add more lemon juice, a little at a time, until the umeboshi paste is sufficiently thinned to mix well in the dressing.
   - Add remaining lemon juice, minced tarragon and garlic, olive oil, and salt. Cover and shake to combine.
4. Pour dressing over salad and mix everything together gently but thoroughly. Taste. Add additional lemon juice, olive oil, and/or salt, if needed.
5. Serve over a bed of salad greens or large sprouts.

NOTES, SUBSTITUTIONS, AND VARIATIONS:

Shelled edamame is often available in the frozen vegetable section of your local grocery store.

Umeboshi plum paste adds a wonderful umami flavor. If it is unavailable, you can simply replace it with adjusted amounts of salt and lemon juice.

Substitute another fresh herb for the tarragon. Other herbs that would work well are basil, mint, and cilantro.

This makes a great layered salad in a jar. Using four pint jars, divide ingredients evenly between them in layers. These can keep, covered, in the refrigerator for several days and be easily taken to work for lunch or out to picnics. Serve with a pile of sprouts on top. Following is a suggested layering order for a version using black beans, navy beans, and small red beans, but you can substitute whatever beans you are using. Layer the ingredients in the following order, starting at the bottom of the jar: edamame, carrots, black beans, cucumbers, half of the dressing, red beans, celery, white beans, remaining dressing.

Brown Rice Tabouli with Summer Veggies

Yield: 6–9 servings (about 6–7 cups)

INGREDIENTS:

1 cup raw brown rice

1 small piece kombu, optional

1–2 cucumbers (about ½ pound), diced into small pieces

3–4 tomatoes (about 1 pound), diced into small pieces

½ red, orange, or yellow bell pepper, diced into small pieces

2 loosely packed cups fresh parsley leaves

1 loosely packed cup fresh mint leaves

2–3 lemons, juiced to make about ⅓ cup lemon juice, or more to taste

2 cloves garlic, peeled and minced

1–2 tablespoons extra-virgin olive oil

1 or more pinches of sea salt, to taste

DIRECTIONS:

1. Rinse brown rice by swishing it in water and pouring through a strainer.
2. Rinse kombu, if using.
3. Put rice and kombu in pot with 2 cups water. Cover pot, then bring to a boil. Turn down heat to keep it at a low boil until all the water is absorbed and the rice is cooked, about 45 minutes. When rice has finished cooking, remove the lid and set the rice aside to cool. You may remove the
kombu if it has not disintegrated; eat or reserve for other uses.
4. **Prepare vegetables and herbs:**
   - Strip mint leaves and tender tops from tough stems. Discard tough stems or reserve for another use. Mince leaves.
   - Remove tough stems of parsley and discard or reserve for another use. Mince leaves and tender stems.
5. Combine cooled rice, veggies, and herbs in a mixing bowl.
6. **Make dressing:**
   - Mix lemon juice, garlic, olive oil, and a pinch or two of salt in a small jar with a fitted lid.
   - Cover jar and shake to combine.
7. Pour dressing over salad and mix everything together thoroughly. Taste. Add additional lemon juice, olive oil, and/or salt, if needed. Mix well and serve.

NOTES, VARIATIONS, AND SUBSTITUTIONS:

Kombu adds umami flavor and also aids in the digestion of the rice.

If the tomatoes are really juicy, your salad may be sloppier than you might like. One way to remedy this is to allow the tomatoes to drain for a little while after dicing and before adding to salad. Be sure to save the yummy fresh tomato juice to drink or add to another dish!

Substitute or add alternative fresh herbs if you'd like, such as cilantro, Vietnamese coriander, dill, or tarragon. Or experiment with different types of mint.

Add fresh corn kernels cut off the cob.

Add pine nuts, sesame seeds, or walnuts.

Corn Pasta Salad with Summer Veggies

Yield: 6–12 servings (about 3 quarts)

INGREDIENTS:

8–10 ounces corn pasta

2 medium eggplants (about 1½ pounds), cut into bite-sized pieces

1½ pounds mixed summer squash, for example zucchini, patty pan, crook-neck, cut into bite-sized pieces

3 tomatoes (about ¾ pound), cut into bite-sized pieces

½ cup Kalamata olives, sliced or coarse-ly chopped

2 tablespoons extra-virgin olive oil, divided

Several pinches of sea salt

2 loosely packed cups fresh basil leaves, coarsely chopped

2 cloves garlic, peeled and minced

3 tablespoons red wine vinegar, or more to taste

DIRECTIONS:

1. Cook pasta until al dente according to directions on package. Drain and rinse with cool water.
2. While pasta is cooking, steam veggies:
3. Place a steamer basket over a covered pot with boiling water. Since the eggplant will take longer, either use two separate pots or put the egg-plant in first and add the squash when the eggplant is partially cooked.
4. Steam the eggplant and squash until just tender but not falling apart.
5. When the veggies are done, remove from heat, remove cover, and set aside to cool.
6. Place the drained pasta in a large mixing or serving bowl; toss with 2 teaspoons of olive oil and a pinch or two of salt. Set aside to cool.
7. **Make dressing:**
   - Mix garlic, remaining 1 tablespoon + 1 teaspoon olive oil, and red wine vinegar in a small jar with a fitted lid.
   - Cover jar and shake to combine.
8. **Assemble salad:**
   - Add prepared veggies to your pasta once everything is cool. Add basil, olives, and salad dressing. Mix gently but thoroughly to com-bine well.
   - Taste and adjust flavor by adding additional red wine vinegar, olive oil, and/or salt as needed.
9. Serve.

SUBSTITUTIONS AND VARIATIONS:

Add a little heat by adding red pepper flakes or a chopped ripe hot pepper such as jalapeño or serrano.

The corn pasta flavor harmonizes very well with the basil and summer veggies, but you can use another type of whole grain pasta if you'd like.

Increase the protein content by substituting quinoa pasta, or by adding cooked or canned garbanzo or kidney beans.

Add lightly steamed Romano-style beans, sliced on the diagonal.

Make a savory sprinkle topping by coarsely grinding sunflower or sesame seeds, almonds, and nutritional yeast together in a blender or food processor.

Substitute another fresh herb for the basil. Other herbs that would work well are cilantro, parsley, and oregano. If using oregano, substantially reduce the quantity.

Lentil Quinoa Salad with Tahini Miso Dressing

Yield: 6–8 servings (about 5–6 cups plus sprouts)

INGREDIENTS:

½ cup French lentils

1 cup quinoa

4¼ cups water, divided

2 green onions, thinly sliced
(use both green and white parts)

1 cup celery, thinly sliced

1 medium carrot, grated

¾ cup fresh parsley leaves, divided

3–4 lemons, juiced to make ½ cup plus
2 tablespoons lemon juice, divided

2–3 cloves garlic, peeled

½ cup raw tahini

1 tablespoon garbanzo bean or other
light miso

¼ teaspoon sea salt, plus more to taste

4 ounces large sprouts such as
sunflower, buckwheat, or pea, or a mix
of large sprouts

DIRECTIONS:

1. Rinse lentils. Cook in 2 cups of water in a covered pot until the lentils are tender but not falling apart. Drain and cool.
2. Rinse quinoa. Cook in a small covered pot with 2 cups of water. Bring to a boil, reduce heat and simmer until all the water is absorbed and the quinoa is tender, about 15–20 minutes. Set aside to cool.
3. Coarsely chop ¼ cup parsley and set the rest aside for the dressing.
4. **Make dressing:**
   - In a blender or food processor, combine tahini, garlic, ¼ cup plus 2 tablespoons lemon juice, miso, reserved parsley, and the remaining ¼ cup water.
   - Process until smooth.
   - Taste and adjust seasonings.
5. When lentils and quinoa have cooled, combine them gently with green onions, celery, carrot, chopped parsley, the remaining ¼ cup lemon juice, and salt. A rubber or silicone spatula is a great tool for gently combining the ingredients without mashing the lentils and quinoa.
6. Taste salad and adjust seasonings.
7. Make a nest of sprouts on a serving platter or broad serving bowl.
8. Mound the salad into the nest.
9. Pour some of the dressing over salad. Reserve the rest to be added to individual servings.
10. Serve.

NOTES, VARIATIONS, AND SUBSTITUTIONS:

Experiment with different herbs in the dressing, e.g. dill, basil, mint.

Add additional veggies such as cucumber, red or yellow bell pepper, and peas.

Substitute baby greens or chopped whole spinach leaves for the sprouts.

Meal on the Table Now Variation:
- If you make extra cooked quinoa and lentils when you are using them for another meal, you can set some aside in the fridge to make this salad.
- Alternatively, you can use canned lentils.
- You can also make the dressing for this salad ahead of time, or use another homemade or store-bought tahini dressing. Then, when you want to make the salad, you can assemble it and get it on the table pretty quickly.

Spring Veggie Brown Rice Tabouli with Mint and Parsley

Yield: 6–8 servings (about 7 cups)

INGREDIENTS:

1 cup raw brown rice

2 cups water

1 small piece kombu, optional

2 green onions, thinly sliced (use both green and white parts)

3–4 stalks celery, minced (enough for about 1 cup sliced)

1 cucumber, diced into small pieces

4 ounces snap peas, cut into ¼-inch slices

½ bunch mint (enough for about ¼ cup)

¼ bunch fresh parsley (enough for about ¼ cup)

¼ cup raw shelled hazelnuts, coarsely chopped

1–2 lemons, juiced to make about ¼ cup lemon juice

2 cloves garlic, peeled and minced

2 tablespoons extra-virgin olive oil

⅛ teaspoon sea salt

DIRECTIONS:

1. Rinse and drain brown rice.
2. Rinse kombu.
3. Put rice, water and kombu, if using, in a pot. Cover pot; bring to a boil. Turn down heat to keep it at a low boil until all the water is absorbed and the rice is cooked, about 45 minutes. When rice has finished cooking, remove the lid and set the rice aside to cool. You may remove the kombu if it has not disintegrated; eat or reserve for other uses.
4. Strip mint leaves and tender tops from tough stems. Discard stems. Mince leaves.
5. Remove tough parsley stems. Discard tough stems or reserve for another use. Mince leaves and tender stems.
6. Combine cooled rice, veggies, herbs, and hazelnuts in a mixing bowl.
7. **Make dressing:**
   - Mix lemon juice, garlic, and olive oil in a small jar with a fitted lid.
   - Cover jar and shake to combine.
8. Pour dressing over salad and mix everything together thoroughly. Taste. Add additional lemon juice, olive oil, and/or salt, if needed; add to salad and mix well.
9. Serve.

NOTES, SUBSTITUTIONS, AND VARIATIONS:

Kombu is a sea vegetable that improves the digestibility of grains and beans when cooked with them. It also adds a little umami flavor.

If mint is unavailable, double the parsley.

Experiment with other spring veggies if you'd like.

This salad keeps well for several days refrigerated. It tends to get less flavorful when stored, so plan to add additional lemon juice when you serve it after a time in the fridge.

Tempeh Wakame Salad

Yield: 4 servings

INGREDIENTS:

1 eight-ounce package of tempeh

1 shallot

1 tablespoon tamari

1 piece kombu, about 4–6 inches long, optional

1 clove garlic, smashed and peeled

1½ cups vegetable stock

Several stalks of celery including leaves, coarsely chopped (about 1 cup)

Several green onions, thinly sliced (use both green and white parts)

¼ cup fresh parsley or cilantro leaves

¼ cup wakame flakes (AKA "instant" wakame)

¼ cup "raw" (untoasted, unsalted) cashews

¼ cup raw pumpkin seeds, hulled

1–2 lemons, juiced to make about about ¼ cup juice

¼ teaspoon sea salt

¼ teaspoon black pepper

¼ cup water, or more for consistency

4–8 ounces watercress or soil-grown sprouts (e.g. buckwheat, sunflower, pea, daikon)

DIRECTIONS:

1. Slice tempeh into ¼-inch slices.
2. Cut one half of the shallot into thick slices and reserve the remaining half for later.
3. Combine tempeh, shallot slices, smashed garlic, tamari, kombu, and vegetable stock in small saucepan. Cover it and bring to a boil; then turn down and leave it simmering until most of the liquid is gone.
4. Prepare remaining veggies and herbs while tempeh is braising:
5. Mince remaining half shallot.
6. Break or cut off tough parsley or cilantro stems and discard. Coarsely chop leaves and tender stems.
7. When the liquid is almost gone from the tempeh, remove the cover and stir the contents, allowing the remaining liquid to evaporate. Remove from heat. If the kombu is tender you can cut it into bite-sized pieces and set it aside to cool with the tempeh.
8. Soak wakame flakes in a large bowl in about 4 cups of water for 8–12 minutes.

9. **Make dressing:**
   - Combine cashews, pumpkin seeds, lemon juice, sea salt, black pepper, and water in a blender or food processor. Process until smooth, scraping down sides as needed.
   - Add more water a little bit at a time if the dressing is too thick.
10. Remove cooled tempeh from fridge and tear into irregular pieces about the size of an almond.
11. Drain wakame.
12. Finish salad by combining prepared veggies, cilantro or parsley, wakame, tempeh, and dressing in a large mixing bowl. Mix well. Taste and adjust lemon juice, pepper, and sea salt.
13. Distribute watercress or sprouts evenly onto four plates.
14. Scoop tempeh wakame salad onto the beds of greens and serve.

NOTES, SUBSTITUTIONS, AND VARIATIONS:

Kombu increases the umami flavor and aids in digestibility; omit if you like.

You can substitute part of a yellow or red onion for the shallot.

Other veggies that would be great additions (or substitutes for the celery) are cucumber, red or yellow bell peppers, and sunchokes.

Add chunks of avocado or use avocado instead of cashews in the dressing.

Chickpea Salad with Roasted Summer Veggies

Yield: 4–6 servings (about 6–7 cups)

INGREDIENTS:

3 cups cooked or 2 15-ounce cans garbanzo beans, drained and rinsed

½ pound eggplant, cut in bite-sized pieces

1 pound summer squash, mixed colors and varieties (for instance zucchini, crookneck, patty pan), cut in bite-sized pieces

2½ tablespoons extra-virgin olive oil, divided

1 or more pinches of sea salt

½ large red, orange, or yellow bell pepper, cut into matchsticks

¼–½ small red onion, thinly sliced

¼ cup sliced Kalamata olives

½ cup fresh basil leaves, plus additional for garnish

1–2 cloves garlic, peeled and minced

½ teaspoon red pepper flakes

1½ tablespoons red wine vinegar

DIRECTIONS:

1. Preheat oven to 450°.
2. Wash eggplant and summer squash. Cut into large bite-sized pieces.
3. Spread eggplant in a single layer without crowding in a baking pan. (Crowding is likely to result in steamed, rather than roasted veggies.) Drizzle 1 teaspoon olive oil over eggplant and sprinkle with a pinch of salt. Toss to distribute oil and salt.
4. Spread squash in a single layer without crowding in another baking pan. Drizzle 1 teaspoon olive oil over squash and sprinkle with a pinch of salt. Toss to distribute oil and salt. If necessary, use more than one pan to avoid crowding.
5. Place prepared veggies in the oven and roast 15 to 20 minutes. Remove from oven and turn veggies over with a spatula, then return to oven for another 5 to 15 minutes until they are roasted enough for your preference. When done, remove veggies and set aside to cool.
6. **While veggies are roasting, make dressing:**
   - Mix garlic, red pepper flakes, remaining olive oil, and red wine vinegar in a small jar with a fitted lid.
   - Cover jar and shake to combine.
7. Set aside a few basil leaves for garnish, and coarsely chop the rest.
8. Combine cooled roasted vegetables, bell pepper, onion, beans, and basil in a bowl.
9. Pour salad dressing over salad. Mix gently to thoroughly combine.
10. Taste and adjust seasonings.
11. Garnish with reserved basil leaves and serve.

NOTES, SUBSTITUTIONS, AND VARIATIONS:

If you are reducing oil in your diet, this recipe works fine with steamed, rather than roasted veggies. Simply place the cut up eggplant in a steamer over boiling water and steam until half done; then add squash and steam until veggies are tender but not falling apart. Or dry roast, using the technique described in the recipe for Double Pea Salad with Roasted Potatoes.

Again, if you are avoiding oils, substitute one of the oil-free dressings in the salad dressing section. Or, make the dressing as above substituting 2 tablespoons vegetable stock or water mixed with 1 teaspoon chia seeds for the olive oil in the dressing.

You can substitute cannellini beans or large white beans for the garbanzos.

This salad will keep well for several days in the refrigerator.

Spring Pasta Salad with Watercress and Shiitake

Yield: 6–10 servings (about 2–2½ quarts)

INGREDIENTS:

12 ounces brown rice pasta spirals or other pasta

3 tablespoons extra-virgin olive oil, divided, or more to taste

a few of pinches of sea salt, divided

8 asparagus spears

4 ounces shiitake mushrooms, sliced

A little bit of vegetable stock

2 small zucchini, thinly sliced

8 ounces snap peas, cut into ¼-inch slices

2–3 green onions, thinly sliced (use both green and white parts)

1 bunch of watercress

¾ cup raw shelled walnuts, broken into several pieces each or coarsely chopped

3 tablespoons red wine vinegar, or more to taste

2–4 cloves garlic, peeled and minced

1 bunch oregano (about ¼ cup minced)

¼ teaspoon umeboshi vinegar, or more to taste

DIRECTIONS:

1. Cook pasta al dente according to directions on package. Drain and rinse with cold water. Place the pasta in a large mixing or serving bowl; toss with 1 tablespoon of olive oil and a pinch or two of salt. Set aside to cool.

2. Snap off tough ends of asparagus spears; reserve for some other use like stock. Cut asparagus into ½-inch pieces. Place in a steamer over boiling water. Cover with lid and steam for about 1 minute. Remove from heat. If the asparagus is bright green and slightly cooked, remove cover to cool. If it needs a little more cooking, leave the cover on for a little bit, being careful not to overcook, then uncover and cool.

3. Dry sauté shiitake mushrooms. Heat a dry cast iron pan over medium high heat. Add the shiitakes and a pinch or two of salt, and dry sauté them by stirring constantly as they heat up. Keep the pan hot enough to cook but not burn them. If they start sticking, add a little bit of vegetable stock or water, being careful just to add a tablespoon or so at a time so the mushrooms will not get soggy. Continue stirring and adding stock as needed until the mushrooms are wilted. Cook out remaining liquid, if any; then remove from heat to cool.

4. Strip leaves off watercress stems by pulling along the stems with your thumb and fingers. You can leave the smaller leaves at the top on tender stems as is. Discard tough stems or reserve for another use such as juice or stock.

5. **Make dressing:**
   - Strip oregano leaves from stems and discard stems. Mince leaves.
   - Mix garlic, oregano, umeboshi vinegar, 2 tablespoons olive oil, and red wine vinegar in a small jar with a fitted lid.
   - Cover jar and shake to combine.

6. **Assemble salad:**
   - Add prepared veggies to your pasta once everything is cool. Add nuts and dressing. Mix gently but thoroughly to combine well.
   - Taste and adjust flavor by adding additional red wine vinegar, olive oil, salt, and/or umeboshi vinegar as needed.

7. Serve.

NOTES, SUBSTITUTIONS, AND VARIATIONS:

This recipe takes a little while to prepare due to the varying preparation methods for the veggies. It makes a generous quantity, however, so if you are making it for an average-sized family or a couple, you will most likely get two or three meals out of it. Also, the combination of veggies is fantastic together!

I include in this recipe a dry sautéing method for the shiitake mushrooms. There are many different perspectives on cooking with oil or even consuming extracted oils. I have recently been experimenting with reducing oil and finding other ways to make foods flavorful. I actually like the dry sautéed shiitake better in this salad than those sautéed in oil. If you want to speed up the recipe a tiny bit and are unconcerned about cooking with olive oil, please feel free to sauté the mushrooms in a little bit of extra-virgin olive oil.

If you are making this salad ahead, consider leaving the watercress out and adding right before serving to keep it fresher.

The watercress makes this salad, in my opinion, and it is also super-healthy. If you cannot get watercress where you live, however, or if you don't like the peppery taste, you can substitute flat-leaf parsley.

You can use another type of whole grain pasta instead of the brown rice pasta.

You can leave out the umeboshi vinegar and use a little more red wine vinegar and a little salt.

If you have nut allergies, you can use 1 cup of cooked or canned kidney or cannelini beans instead of the walnuts.

Make a winter veggie pasta salad by substituting lightly steamed broccoli and roasted winter squash for the snap peas, asparagus and zucchini. Substitute parsley for the watercress.

Composed Salads

Fennel, Cucumber, and Watermelon Radish Salad with Creamy Cashew Dip

Yield: 6 servings

INGREDIENTS:

1 cup "raw" (untoasted, unsalted) cashews (note: these get soaked overnight)

2–3 small heads Belgian endive or baby bok choy

1 cucumber, thinly sliced on a strong diagonal

½ large watermelon radish or a whole small one, quartered, then thinly sliced into quarter moons

1 fennel bulb, thinly sliced

1–2 lemons, juiced to make about ¼ cup lemon juice

Pinch of sea salt

¼ cup water, or more for consistency

Edible flowers such as chive flowers, nasturtiums, calendulas, marigolds, edible chrysanthemums, or alyssum, for garnish

DIRECTIONS:

1. Soak the cashews in two or three times their volume of water for 6–24 hours. Drain and rinse well.
2. Remove all endive or bok choy leaves from their heads; set aside.
3. On a large platter, arrange your endive or baby bok choy leaves around the outside like the petals of a flower. Lay the cucumber slices over the greens, like the next inner ring of petals, overlapping and going around more than once if necessary to use up all the remaining cucumber slices.
4. Next, use the watermelon radish slices to create the next ring of petals. At this point, there will be a fairly small empty circle in the middle of your platter. Fill it up with the fennel slices, piling them nicely to make a flower center.
5. Garnish the salad with edible flowers.
6. **Make the dip**
   - In a blender or food processor, process soaked cashews, lemon juice, salt, and water until smooth. Add a little more water if necessary for processing.
   - Taste and adjust seasonings
7. Serve the salad and pass the dip!

NOTES, SUBSTITUTIONS, AND VARIATIONS:

If you have a mandoline, use it to slice the vegetables. If not, a sharp knife will also work.

If you cannot find watermelon radishes, you can substitute mild turnip or rutabaga slices, stained pink with the juice of a beet.

Substitute a different dressing such as Creamy Tarragon or Tahini Dill.

Rainbow Mandala Salad

Yield: 4–6 servings (about 6–8 cups)

INGREDIENTS:

1 red bell pepper, cut into matchsticks

1 yellow bell pepper, cut into matchsticks

4–5 large Roma-style green beans, thinly sliced on the diagonal

1 cucumber, thinly sliced

2 cobs of corn

3 small heirloom tomatoes in a variety of colors, cut into thin wedges

1 large carrot, spiralized or finely grated

Edible flowers for garnish, optional

DIRECTIONS:

1. Shuck and de-silk corn; cut kernels off the cobs.
2. Pile the corn in a circle onto the center of a large platter, leaving space around the edges of the corn circle.
3. Pile carrots in the center of the corn, leaving a wide rim of corn showing.
4. Place the cucumbers around the edge of the platter in two overlapping rows, overlapping the top of the corn circle.
5. Arrange the other veggies in concentric circles on top of the salad in a pleasing arrangement.
6. Add edible flowers for garnish.
7. Serve with dressing on the side.

NOTES, SUBSTITUTIONS, AND VARIATIONS:

This is a salad to make in the summer. Substitute other seasonal veggies to make a mandala in other seasons. For instance, in the winter use a variety of colors of cauliflower cut into florets, vari-colored carrot and beet sticks, winter greens, and winter flowers such as calendula and mustard.

If you want all the colors of the rainbow, use purple and blue flowers as I did. Or use purple beans, bell pepper, cauliflower, or red cabbage for the purple. Please let me know if you figure out a great blue vegetable to add!

Use the vegetables and design of this salad as a starting point, and create your own mandala using whatever seasonal raw veggies you can get, cut into the shapes you choose and arranged in your own design. I'd love to see a photo of your creation!

Suggested dressings are Tahini Dill, Avocado Lemon, or Creamy Tarragon.

Cucumber Salsa and White Bean Stuffed Avocados

Yield: 6 servings

INGREDIENTS:

1 large cucumber, chopped into large chunks

1–3 chiles, mild to moderate heat

¼ small yellow onion, cut in several pieces

1–3 green onions, cut into several pieces (use both green and white parts)

¼ bunch cilantro

¼ bunch fresh mint

1 lime, juiced to make 2 tablespoons lime juice (or more to taste)

1–2 cloves garlic, peeled and coarsely chopped

Pinch of sea salt, or more to taste

1½ cups cooked or 1 15-ounce can white beans, drained and rinsed

2 large or 3 small ripe avocados

4–8 ounces of mixed sprouts such as sunflower, buckwheat, pea, radish, etc.

DIRECTIONS:

1. Remove chile stems and cut in quarters. Remove some seeds and white pith for a medium spicy salsa, or leave all seeds and pith if you want it spicier. If removing seeds, reserve some for adjusting heat later.
2. Strip leaves from mint stems.
3. Cut or tear off tough cilantro stems.
4. Combine cucumber, chiles, both kinds of onions, garlic, herbs, lime juice, and a pinch of salt in the container of a blender or food processor. Pulse process until you have a coarse salsa consistency. Pause to scrape down bowl sides if needed.
5. Taste for spiciness. Add some of the reserved chile seeds if you want more heat, and process briefly to combine.
6. Dump salsa into a mixing bowl, and gently mix beans into salsa.
7. Taste and adjust salt and lime juice.
8. If using small avocados, halve lengthwise. If large avocados, cut into thirds lengthwise. Carefully remove pits and peels.
9. Divide the sprouts evenly across six plates.
10. Place a half or third avocado on each sprout bed, cavity side up.
11. Spoon the salsa into and onto the avocado halves.
12. Serve.

NOTES, SUBSTITUTIONS, AND VARIATIONS:

Substitute another fresh herb for the cilantro. Other herbs that would work well are parsley and basil.

Use baby greens if sprouts are not available.

Double the cilantro if mint is not available.

Meal on the Table Now Variation:
- Substitute store-bought green salsa for the homemade salsa.
- Serve with extra lime wedges on the side.

Eight-Layer Raw Pasta Salad with Three Sauces

Yield: 6–10 servings (about 8–10 cups)

NOTE: This salad takes a lot of time, but it tastes and looks fabulous!

INGREDIENTS:

3 ounces unsalted dried tomatoes

2½–3 medium zucchini, divided

2–3 crookneck squash

3–4 medium cucumbers

2–4 carrots

Sea salt

¼ cup + 2 tablespoons raw pumpkin seeds

¼ cup + 2 tablespoons extra-virgin olive oil, divided

5–6 cloves garlic, peeled and coarsely minced, divided

1 bunch basil (about 1–2 cups fresh basil leaves, lightly packed)

¼ teaspoon black pepper

3 tablespoons nutritional yeast

1½ teaspoons garbanzo bean or other light miso

Dash of umeboshi vinegar

½ lemon, zested then juiced to make about 1 tablespoon lemon juice

1–2 tablespoons fresh thyme leaves

1 cup pitted Kalamata olives

1 cup raw shelled walnuts

1–2 teaspoons fresh rosemary leaves

4 tablespoons raw shelled pine nuts, divided

¼ teaspoon umeboshi plum paste

2–4 ounces mixed sprouts

DIRECTIONS:

1. Soak dried tomatoes in double their volume of water.
2. **Make veggie pasta using a spiralizer:**
   - If your spiralizer leaves a little bit of veggie unspiralized, set aside half of a zucchini for the pesto. If your spiralizer does not leave bits unspiralized, set aside one zucchini for the pesto.
   - Spiralize veggies individually, putting each in a separate bowl or colander. As you complete each veggie, sprinkle several pinches of sea salt on the pasta and gently mix it into the pasta. Set aside.
   - If your spiralizer leaves a little piece of each veggie unspiralized, reserve the pieces of squash for the pesto and the carrot and cucumber pieces for another use.
   - When all the pasta is made and salted, begin draining the excess water out of each type of pasta, beginning with the one that has been salted the longest. Press gently to remove excess liquid. It is not necessary to get the pasta super dry.

3. **Make pesto as follows:**
   - In a food processor, grind the pumpkin seeds into a fairly fine texture.
   - If you have squash ends from spiralizing, use these plus one more half a zucchini in your pesto. If you do not have squash ends, use a whole zucchini for the pesto. Cut the zucchini into ¾-inch chunks.
   - Place squash pieces left from spiralizing, zucchini chunks, 2½ tablespoons olive oil, one-third of the minced garlic, basil leaves, black pepper, nutritional yeast, miso, and a dash or two of umeboshi vinegar in the food processor with the ground pumpkin seeds.
   - Process until everything is well combined and is a coarse pesto texture. You may have to pause and scrape down several times.
   - Taste and adjust seasonings. Set pesto aside.

4. **Make tapenade as follows:**
   - Strip thyme leaves and tender tops from stems.
   - In a food processor, combine pitted Kalamata olives, one-third of the minced garlic, walnuts, thyme leaves and tops, 1½ tablespoons olive oil, and the lemon zest and juice.
   - Process until ingredients are chopped into a coarse-textured tapenade. You may have to pause and scrape down several times.
   - Taste and adjust seasonings. Set tapenade aside.

5. **Make dry tomato sauce as follows:**
   - Remove tomatoes from soaking water and chop. Reserve soaking water.
   - Strip rosemary leaves from stems and chop.
   - In a food processor, combine chopped tomatoes, remaining third of the minced garlic, remaining 2 tablespoons olive oil, 3 tablespoons pine nuts, rosemary, umeboshi paste, and ½ cup of the tomato soaking water.
   - Process until ingredients are well mixed and chopped and you have a coarse-textured, thick sauce. You may have to pause and scrape down several times. Add additional soaking water if needed.
   - Taste and adjust seasonings. Set sauce aside.

6. **Assemble the salad** by layering the components in a large (at least 2 quarts), clear glass bowl in the following order, starting at the bottom:
   - Zucchini pasta
   - Tomato sauce
   - Crookneck pasta
   - Pesto
   - Carrot pasta
   - Tapenade
   - Cucumber pasta
   - Sprouts sprinkled with remaining pine nuts.

7. If you choose to make salad jars, use 4–5 pint-sized jars and layer as above.

NOTES, VARIATIONS, AND SUBSTITUTIONS:

If you avoid extracted oils, leave the olive oil out and make the following changes:
- Add half an avocado to the pesto.
- Remove the oil from the tapenade recipe; use other ingredients as is. Or add a tiny bit of veggie stock if it is too thick. Add additional lemon juice to boost the flavor if you'd like.
- Eliminate oil in the tomato sauce; use additional tomato soaking liquid if needed.

If you cannot find unsalted dried tomatoes, use the salted kind but eliminate the umeboshi plum paste from the tapenade.

Experiment with different basils for the pesto, such as lemon basil or Thai basil. Or use cilantro or parsley instead of basil.

Add a little prepared cultured nut cheese to the pesto.

Try different nuts for the tapenade, or instead of pumpkin seeds in the pesto.

Make it a little spicy by adding a small red chile to the tomato sauce.

Meal on the Table Now Variation:
- To make this more quickly, use store-bought tapenade, vegan pesto, and sundried tomato sauce.
- Simplify further by reducing the number of pasta veggies to one or two. Spiralize the pasta, salt and drain it, then assemble as above.

Salad Dressings

Basic Balsamic Vinaigrette

Yield: about ½ cup

INGREDIENTS:

Fresh oregano leaves and tender tops (enough for 1 packed tablespoon)

2 cloves garlic, peeled and minced

3 tablespoons extra-virgin olive oil

¼ cup balsamic vinegar

¼ teaspoon liquid lecithin, optional

DIRECTIONS:

1. Remove oregano leaves and tender tops from stems and discard stems or reserve for another use. Mince leaves and tender tops.
2. Mix all ingredients in a small jar with a fitted lid. Cover jar and shake to combine and serve.

NOTES, SUBSTITUTES, AND VARIATIONS:

The lecithin is a natural emulsifier. It will help the oil and vinegar to mix together and stay that way. If you do not have lecithin, just be sure to shake well immediately before pouring on salad.

This dressing keeps well for several days or more at room temperature. Do not refrigerate as the oil will thicken, creating a barrier to proper emulsification.

Substitute another fresh herb for the oregano, or leave the herbs out altogether. Other herbs that work well include thyme, rosemary, basil, and tarragon.

Avocado Lemon Dressing

Yield: about ¾ cup

NOTE: This simple dressing is best consumed on the day it is made; the avocado tends to oxidize over time, so make in small batches that you can use up. See photo page 102.

INGREDIENTS:

1 medium avocado, peeled and pitted

2–3 lemons, juiced to make about ¼ cup

1–2 tablespoons leaves of fresh herbs such as lemon thyme, basil, or parsley, optional

Sufficient water for consistency

DIRECTIONS:

1. Combine avocado, lemon juice, and herb leaves and tops in blender or food processor. Process until smooth. Add water, a teaspoon or two at a time, until it is still thick but pourable.

2. Alternatively, you can mash the avocado in a bowl, chop the herbs, and combine all ingredients by hand, adding water to make the desired consistency.

Tahini Dill Dressing

Yield: about 1⅓ cup

INGREDIENTS:

½ cup raw tahini

½ cup fresh dill leaves

2–3 lemons, juiced to make about ⅓ cup lemon juice

1 teaspoon umeboshi plum paste

⅜ cup water, or more for consistency

DIRECTIONS:

1. Cut off bottom part of dill stems if they are tough.
2. Combine all ingredients in a blender or food processor. Process until smooth.
3. Add additional water, a teaspoon or two at a time, until it is still thick but pourable.
4. Taste and adjust seasonings.

NOTES, SUBSTITUTES, AND VARIATIONS:

This dressing keeps well for several days or more in the refrigerator.

You can substitute other herbs for the dill. If using annual or biennial herbs such as basil, parsley, or cilantro, you can use as much as ½ cup of the leaves and tender tops. If using perennials such as lemon thyme, rosemary, or oregano, use much less, since these herbs tend to be much more strongly flavored. For example, the strong flavor of rosemary suggests that ½–1 teaspoon would be adequate. For thyme or oregano, 1–2 tablespoons would be plenty.

You can substitute another salty substance such as tamari, liquid aminos, or salt for the umeboshi. If doing this, increase the lemon juice a little bit.

Creamy Tarragon Dressing

Yield: about 2 cups

INGREDIENTS:

1 cup "raw" (untoasted, unsalted) cashews (note: these get soaked overnight)

1 lemon, juiced to make about 2–3 tablespoons, or more to taste

¼ cup fresh tarragon leaves

½ cup water, or more for consistency

DIRECTIONS:

1. Soak cashews in double or triple their volume of water for 6–24 hours. Drain cashews.
2. Combine all ingredients in blender or food processor. Process until smooth.
3. If it is too thick, add water, a teaspoon or two at a time, until it is still thick but pourable.
4. Taste and adjust seasonings.
5. Serve.

NOTES, SUBSTITUTIONS, AND VARIATIONS:

It is optional to soak the cashews. The dressing is creamier if the nuts are soaked, and you will get the yield noted above. If you do not have time to soak them, use as is and adjust water accordingly to make the texture you want. The yield may be considerably less.

Although fresh tarragon is amazing, it can be challenging to find. Feel free to experiment with different herbs instead. For instance, try cilantro, basil, parsley, mint, or mint. Or use a smaller quantity of oregano, rosemary, thyme, or sage.

You can substitute macadamia nuts for the cashews for a delightful twist!

Store leftovers in a covered container in the refrigerator and use within a few days.

Oil-Free Parsley Lemon Dressing

Yield: about ⅝ cup

INGREDIENTS:

¼ cup vegetable stock or water

¼ teaspoon psyllium husks

2–3 lemons, juiced to make about ¼ cup lemon juice

Fresh parsley, enough for 2 tablespoons of leaves

2 cloves garlic, peeled and minced

DIRECTIONS:

1. Combine stock or water with psyllium husks in a small jar and set it aside to gel.
2. Remove parsley leaves and tender tops from stems and discard stems or reserve for another use. Mince leaves and tender tops.
3. Add all ingredients to the thickened stock or water/psyllium mixture. Stir well to combine.
4. Serve.

NOTES, SUBSTITUTES, AND VARIATIONS:

This dressing keeps well for several days or more in the refrigerator.

Substitute another fresh herb for the parsley. Other herbs that would work well are cilantro, dill, and basil.

Avocado Tahini Lime Dressing

Yield: about ¾ cup

NOTE: This dressing is best consumed on the day it is made; the avocado tends to oxidize over time, so make in small batches that you can use up.

INGREDIENTS:

½ large avocado, peeled and pitted

1 lime, juiced to make about 2 tablespoons lime juice

1 clove garlic, peeled and coarsely chopped

2 tablespoons raw sesame tahini

¼ teaspoon umeboshi vinegar

Water, for consistency

DIRECTIONS:

Combine all ingredients in a blender or food processor; process until smooth. Add water, a teaspoon or two at a time, until it is still thick but pourable.

Alternatively, mash the avocado in a bowl, mince the garlic, and combine all ingredients by hand, again adding water to make the desired consistency.

Oil-Free Balsamic Vinaigrette

Yield: about ⅜ cup

INGREDIENTS:

2 tablespoons vegetable stock or water

1 teaspoon chia seeds

Fresh thyme leaves and tender tops, enough for 1 packed tablespoon

2 cloves garlic, peeled and minced

¼ cup balsamic vinegar

DIRECTIONS:

1. Combine stock or water with chia seeds in a small jar; set aside to gel.
2. Remove thyme leaves and tender tops from stems. Discard stems or reserve for another use. Mince leaves and tender tops.
3. Add all ingredients to the thickened stock or water chia mixture. Stir well to combine and serve.

NOTES, SUBSTITUTES, AND VARIATIONS:

This dressing keeps well for several days or more in the refrigerator.

Substitute another fresh herb for the thyme, or leave the herbs out altogether. Other herbs that would work well are chives, rosemary, oregano, and parsley.

Oil-Free Chile Lime Poppy Seed Dressing

Yield: about ½ cup

INGREDIENTS:

3 tablespoons vegetable stock or water

1 teaspoon chia seeds

1 green or red chile, stemmed and minced

1 lime, juiced to make 2 tablespoons lime juice

1 teaspoon poppy seeds

DIRECTIONS:

1. Combine stock or water with chia seeds in a small jar; set aside to gel.
2. Add all ingredients to the thickened stock or water/chia seed mixture.
3. Stir well to combine and serve.

NOTES, SUBSTITUTES, AND VARIATIONS:

This dressing keeps well for several days or more in the refrigerator.

If you want a less spicy dressing, remove all or part of the seeds and pith from the chile.

If you want a completely mild dressing, substitute part of a red or yellow bell pepper for the chile.

Creamy Dried Tomato and Basil Dressing

Yield: about 1½ cups

INGREDIENTS:

½ cup "raw" (untoasted, unsalted) cashews (note: these get soaked overnight)

¼ cup unsalted dried tomatoes (packed)

⅞ cup water, or more for consistency, divided

1 tablespoon umeboshi vinegar

¼ cup fresh basil leaves

DIRECTIONS:

1. Soak cashews in double or triple their volume of water for 6–24 hours.
2. Drain cashews and discard water or reserve for another use.
3. Soak tomatoes in ½ cup water for 10 minutes or more to soften.
4. Combine cashews, tomatoes and their soaking water, the remaining ⅜ cup water, and the umeboshi vinegar in blender or food processor. Process until smooth. If it is too thick, add water, a teaspoon or two at a time, until it is still thick but pourable.
5. Coarsely chop basil leaves.
6. Add basil to dressing mixture and process briefly to incorporate.
7. Serve.

NOTES, SUBSTITUTIONS, AND VARIATIONS:

Store leftovers in a covered container in the refrigerator and use within a few days.

It is optional to soak the cashews. The dressing is creamier if the nuts are soaked, and you will get the yield noted above. If you do not have time to soak them, use as is and adjust water accordingly to make the texture you want. The yield will be considerably less.

If you cannot find unsalted dried tomatoes, use salted ones and leave out the umeboshi.

If you do not have umeboshi vinegar, substitute lemon juice and a tiny bit of salt.

Substitute another fresh herb or herbs for the basil. Other herbs that would work well include cilantro, oregano, or rosemary. (Use less of the herbs if using a strongly flavored perennial such as oregano or rosemary.)

Fruit Salads

Apricots and Peaches with Cardamom and Coconut Yogurt

Yield: 3–4 servings (about 5 cups)

INGREDIENTS:

2 ½ pounds peaches and apricots, sliced

1 teaspoon decorticated cardamom seeds

1 cup plain coconut yogurt, unsweetened or lightly sweetened

DIRECTIONS:

1. Coarsely grind cardamom seeds in a spice grinder.
2. Sprinkle cardamom over fruit. Mix together gently but thoroughly. A rubber spatula makes a good tool for mixing soft fruit without mashing it.
3. Add coconut yogurt and mix again.
4. Serve.

SUBSTITUTIONS:

If you do not have a spice grinder (or a coffee or seed grinder), you can put the cardamom seeds in whole for a nice "pop!" Or you can use purchased ground cardamom and adjust the amount to suit your taste.

If peaches and apricots are out of season, substitute seasonal fruits such as pears, kiwis, and strawberries.

If you are fortunate enough to live in an area where tropical fruits grow, this recipe is also fabulous with mangoes, papayas, bananas, and pineapple instead of the temperate climate fruits.

Minted Fruit Salad with Coconut and Chia

Yield: 3–4 servings (about 5 cups)

INGREDIENTS:

¼ cup coconut water, either from a young coconut or packaged

¼ cup fresh coconut meat (or substitute shredded unsweetened coconut)

2 ½ pounds mixed fruit such as peaches, apricots, nectarines, pears, strawberries, cherries, raspberries, blueberries, etc.

1 lime, juiced to make about 2 tablespoons of lime juice

1 tablespoon chia seeds

¼ cup loosely packed fresh mint leaves

DIRECTIONS:

1. If you have a whole young coconut, open it up and drain out the coconut water; reserve water. Scoop out the coconut meat. Set aside.
2. In a small jar with a fitted lid, combine ¼ cup coconut water and chia seeds. Set it aside to thicken.
3. Prepare fruit as appropriate. For example, slice stone fruits, halve or quarter strawberries, remove stems and pits from cherries, cut pears into bite-sized pieces.
4. Cut thin strips out the coconut meat to make a ¼ cup.
5. Coarsely chop mint leaves.
6. Place fruit, chopped mint, and coconut strips (or shredded coconut) in a bowl.
7. Add lime juice to coconut/chia mixture to make dressing. Cover and shake to combine.
8. Pour dressing over salad. Mix everything together gently but thoroughly. A rubber spatula makes a good tool for mixing soft fruit without mashing it.
9. Serve.

Mixed Berry Salad with Tarragon

Yield: 2–3 servings (about 3 cups)

INGREDIENTS:

1¼ cups blackberries, cut in halves if large

1¼ cups strawberries, cut in halves or quarters

1¼ cups blueberries

1 tablespoon fresh tarragon leaves

1 teaspoon balsamic vinegar

2 teaspoons coconut sugar

DIRECTIONS:

1. Strip tarragon leaves off of stems and coarsely chop.
2. Combine all ingredients in a bowl and mix well.
3. Cover and refrigerate for several hours or overnight, then serve.

NOTES, VARIATIONS, AND SUBSTITUTIONS:

Yum!

Preparing this recipe in advance allows flavors to mingle.

Use alternate berries if the three named berries are not available.

Use basil instead of tarragon.

Grapefruit and Avocado with Lemon Thyme and Pistachios

Yield: 3–5 servings

INGREDIENTS:

2 pink grapefruit

1 large or 2 small avocados, cut into large bite-sized chunks

1 teaspoon fresh lemon thyme leaves and tender tops

2 tablespoons raw shelled pistachios

DIRECTIONS:

1. Using a knife, cut the peel off grapefruit. Separate sections and cut or peel the membranes off. Cut sections in half.
2. Strip lemon thyme leaves and tender tops from tough stems. Discard stems or reserve for another use. Mince leaves and tops.
3. Mix grapefruit, avocado, and thyme together gently but thoroughly. A rubber spatula works well for mixing soft fruit without mashing it.
4. Sprinkle pistachios on top and serve.

NOTES, SUBSTITUTIONS, AND VARIATIONS:

The noted yield is based on the size of the ingredients I used. The quantity varies tremendously depending on the size of your grapefruit.

Mangos are a great addition. In late summer where I live we have access to Keitt mangos grown in California and I love to add them to this salad!

Substitute another fresh herb for the lemon thyme. Others that would work well are mint, tarragon, basil, and sage.

Cherry Berry Basil Salad with Pomegranate Chia Dressing

Yield: 4–6 servings (about 5–6 cups)

INGREDIENTS:

½ cup pomegranate juice

2 tablespoons chia seeds

6 cups assorted pitted cherries and berries, cut in halves if large

8–12 large fresh basil leaves

DIRECTIONS:

1. **Make dressing:**
   - Mix pomegranate juice and chia seeds and set aside to gel.
   - Stir occasionally.
2. Chiffonade basil leaves (see directions below).
3. Place all fruit in a bowl.
4. Pour dressing over fruit.
5. Sprinkle most of the basil on the salad. Reserve some for garnish.
6. Using a rubber spatula, gently but thoroughly mix the salad ingredients together.
7. Sprinkle reserved basil strips on top.
8. Serve.

NOTES, SUBSTITUTIONS, AND VARIATIONS:

To chiffonade the basil leaves, stack the leaves a few at a time, roll them tightly from the stem of the leaves to the tips, then cut across the roll to make long, thin strips.

Substitute other spring and summer fruits for the cherries and berries if you'd like.

Experiment with different basils such as lemon basil and opal basil.

Use mint instead of basil.

Try alternate fruit juices.

If you do not have a cherry pitter, you can cut them in half to remove the pits, or you can use a clean hairpin to push the pit out from the stem end to the bottom.

Berry Salad Jars with Coconut Mint Chutney

Yield: 4 servings (about 4 cups)

INGREDIENTS:

1 lime, juiced to make about 1 tablespoon lime juice

Fresh mint (enough for 2 tablespoons mint leaves plus a few for garnish)

1 cup shredded unsweetened coconut

½ cup water

4 cups assorted berries, cut in halves if large

DIRECTIONS:

1. **Make coconut mint chutney:**
   - Strip mint leaves from stems.
   - Combine lime juice, mint leaves, coconut, and water in blender or food processor. Process until it becomes a coarse paste.
2. **Assemble salad:**
   - Find four clear glass jars or other containers that have a capacity of approximately 1 cup each.
   - Layer berries and chutney in an order that looks pleasing, given the color combination of your fruit.
3. Garnish with a mint leaf or cluster of small leaves.
4. Serve

NOTES, SUBSTITUTIONS, AND VARIATIONS:

Instead of berries you can use the chutney and this same technique with other fruits such as whole, pitted cherries or bite-sized pieces of peaches, mangos, apricots, and/or pears.

If you don't want a layered jar salad, simply mix the berries together in a serving bowl and serve the chutney on the side.

Strawberry Apricot Salad with Avocado Lime Cream

Yield: 4 servings (about 4–5 cups)

INGREDIENTS:

½ cup "raw" (untoasted, unsalted) cashews (note: these get soaked overnight)

1 large avocado, peeled and pitted

1 lime, juiced to make about 2 tablespoons lime juice

½ cup water, or more for texture

1 ½ pints strawberries (about 2 cups chopped)

1 pound apricots (about 2 cups chopped)

Additional fruit for garnish

DIRECTIONS:

1. Soak cashews in double or triple their volume of water for 6–24 hours.
2. **Make avocado lime cream:**
   - Remove pit and peel from avocado.
   - Combine lime juice, avocado, soaked cashews, and water in a blender or food processor. Process until smooth, adding a little more water if necessary.
3. Remove stems and leaves of strawberries. Very coarsely chop berries up with a knife, or alternatively, cut them in halves and coarsely chop with a brief pulse processing in a food processor.
4. Remove apricot pits; then chop with a knife or food processor as you did with the berries.
5. **Assemble salad:**
   - Find four clear glass jars or other containers that have a capacity of approximately one cup each.
   - Layer berries and avocado lime cream in an order that looks pleasing to you. Use a pastry bag to pipe the avocado lime cream into the jars, if you have one. Or simply use a spoon.
   - End the layering with a dollop or squirt of avocado lime cream.
   - Garnish with a few slices of fruit.
6. Serve.

VARIATIONS AND SUBSTITUTIONS:

If apricots are not in season, substitute orange- or yellow-fleshed peaches or nectarines.

Try other fruit combinations with striking color contrasts or complements.

Use unsoaked cashews if you are pressed for time. You may have to add additional water and processing time to get it smooth, and the yield may be different.

Skip the jars and layer in a small glass serving bowl instead. Or layer it in champagne or wine glasses of a similar capacity.

If you want a dessert instead of a salad, add a few pitted, chopped, soft medjool dates to the avocado lime cream before processing.

Additional Resources

Support for the Journey

START WHERE YOU ARE

It may be a cliché, but it's true, every journey starts with the first step. Start your journey where you are. If you are already a committed vegan, thank you for your contributions to humanity, non-human animals, and the planet. Maybe the first step on your next leg of the journey is to increase the vitality of your diet by eating more raw and fermented veggies, or maybe it's to get more educated in order to be a better activist. Or perhaps you are a person who wants to go vegan and you need additional information and support. Or you are committed to your current choice to be an omnivore, but have decided to reap the many benefits available to you, humanity, the animals, and the earth by decreasing animal products and increasing plants in your diet. Wherever you are on the spectrum, this final section of the book has resources to support your next step, and the one after that, and the one after that....

Homemade Ingredients

It's wonderful to be able to incorporate ingredients you have made yourself into your culinary creations. Here are instructions for making a few ingredients. Future books in the Tastes Like Love series will further develop this theme.

VEGETABLE STOCK

It is incredibly easy to make your own vegetable stock. When you are preparing food, save flavorful vegetable trimmings you would otherwise discard for making stock. Suggestions of great items for stock are trimmings from the ends of onions, celery, carrots, broccoli, cauliflower, parsnips, and fennel; stems from herbs such as parsley, dill, basil, oregano, rosemary; midribs from kale, collards, and chard; leaves of root crops such as radishes, turnips, beets, and carrots (not too much carrot tops, as they can be bitter); husks, silk, and cobs from corn; mushroom stems; etc.

If you use a lot of vegetables, enough material should accumulate that you can collect the trimmings for a week or so and store in a sealed container or plastic bag in the refrigerator until you are ready to make the stock. If you will be making the stock at longer intervals or it takes a lot of time to accumulate enough ingredients, it is better to store in the freezer.

When you are ready to make stock, plunge your ingredients in a large bowl of water to clean; then trim off anything that looks rotten or otherwise completely unappetizing. Place trimmings and fresh water in a large covered pot and bring to a boil on the stove. Turn down to simmer, then leave simmering for several hours, or until the stock is flavorful and the vegetable trimmings have lost most of their flavor. Strain and store in jars in the fridge until ready for use.

A few notes: Onion skins give the stock a lovely color, but too many onion skins cause bitterness so I minimize them. Making single ingredient stocks, or stocks with finite ingredients and using them strategically is wonderful. For instance, when you make the Corn Salad with Chipotle and Lime recipe, you will have a lot of corn husks, cobs, and silk. If you use just these for stock, you will have a light, sweet stock that would be great for a cream soup made with cashew or almond milk and veggies.

FROZEN HERBS

To preserve fresh herbs in season for use in the winter, wash your herbs, then strip leaves and tender stems and tops from tough stems. Set aside the stems for your stock making. Put the leaves, tender stems, and tops in a blender or food processor with a small amount of water—enough to process, but not so much as to make the mixture super diluted. Process until herbs are well chopped. Pour the mixture into an ice cube tray and freeze. When frozen, pop the cubes out and store in labeled, sealed containers or plastic zip-type bags in the freezer. When you are ready to use in hot food, simply take out a cube or two and drop into your pot. For uncooked food uses, you will need to thaw the cubes.

UMEBOSHI PLUMS AND VINEGAR

In Japan, there is a special fruit for making umeboshi. It is plum-like, but not a plum. These little fruits, when fermented, yield ingredients that lend a bright perk to so many dishes that I love to have plenty on hand. The store-bought ume are very expensive, and plums are inexpensive or even free in season where I live, so I started experimenting with making my own.

Here is a quick methodology for making umeboshi-style plums and vinegar out of plums you can find in your area. I will include a full recipe in my upcoming book: Tastes Like Love: Ferment the Garden. Choose plums that are approaching ripe but not yet soft. Make sure they have intact skins—no holes, cracks, or significant blemishes. Remove the stems carefully with a toothpick, being sure not to puncture the skin. Clean the plums by submerging in water to which you have added a splash of white vinegar or vodka. Rinse the plums in fresh water.

Layer the plums with salt equal to 10–12% of their weight in a clean crock or large jar. For example, if you have 20 ounces of plums, use 2–2.4 ounces of salt. If you have access to shiso (AKA "perilla") leaves, wash and pound some of those; add to the plums and salt while layering. Place a clean weight on top of the plums. The weight should be at least half as heavy as the plums, for instance in the 20-ounce example, you would use a weight that is at least 10 ounces. A zip-type plastic bag of water makes a convenient weight because it fits well into any container. You can also use the stones that come with your crock, if you have them, and add jars of water on top to get to the appropriate weight. Cover the crock or jar using an air lock, if you have one. If you don't have an airlock, cover but don't seal, as gases produced in fermentation need to escape. Leave in a safe spot where it won't be disturbed for 2–4 months while fermenting.

After fermentation, remove the plums from the brine. Put the brine in jars (this is the "vinegar") and dry the plums by putting in the sun if you live in a climate with plenty of sun, or by putting in a dehydrator. I store both my plums and vinegar in the fridge long term, though they are shelf stable for some time.

Glossary of Special Ingredients:

Following are descriptions of some of the less common ingredients in the recipes. I welcome you to contact me with questions about these or other ingredients, if you'd like.

Arame: A type of kelp that is generally shredded, cooked, and dried before packaging. The dark strands of arame processed in this way rehydrate fairly quickly.

Chia Seeds: Tiny, nutrient dense seeds that have the capacity to soak up many times their volume of liquid. Chia seeds are often used for thickening things, as they make a nice gel rather quickly when added to water. They do not work as well for highly acidic liquids, so it is recommended to mix them with water and let them sit for a little bit before adding strongly acidic liquids.

Coconut Sugar: A crystallized sugar that is created by collecting the sap of a coconut flower and evaporating the liquid. Since it is minimally processed, there are some nutrients in it. I use a very small amount of it at times, but it is still sugar and not something I recommend eating a lot of!

Decorticated Cardamom Seeds: The seeds of the spice cardamom come in pods. You can buy the seeds in pods and throw the whole thing in chai. If you are going to use cardamom in food, however, it is best to either take the seeds out of the pods yourself or buy them already removed, or "decorticated."

Dried Chipotle Peppers: Chipotle peppers are jalapeños that have been smoked for a very long time. They can often be found dried in stores in the section with other dried peppers.

Hijiki (AKA "hiziki"): A very dark-colored seaweed that grows in thin strands and is steamed and dried before packaging for sale. Soak hijiki for 15 minutes or longer before using in soups, salads, or other dishes.

Kombu: A type of kelp with thick, dense leaves, kombu is tasty and tender if well cooked. It is often added to grains and legumes while cooking to improve digestibility and flavor.

Live, Fermented Sauerkraut (AKA "raw sauerkraut," "fresh kraut," etc.): The recipes in this book that include sauerkraut are intended to be made with sauerkraut that has not been heated or canned. Live, fermented, raw kraut is full of gut-healthy probiotics, and heat destroys them. If the kraut is being sold in a refrigerated case, most likely it is live and fermented. If it's sold on an unrefrigerated grocery shelf in a sealed jar or can, it is most certainly not live, raw sauerkraut.

Miso: A paste made by fermenting soybeans or other beans and grains, miso is salty and richly flavored. I recommend buying miso that has not been pasteurized. Miso is not a raw food, since the beans and grains are cooked before fermenting, but the process of fermentation does create live probiotics in the final product. In order to preserve this quality and reap the benefits from it, don't cook the miso. Instead, add it to foods after removing them from the stove. Or use in cold foods like some of the salad dressings in this book.

Nutritional Yeast: Unlike brewer's yeast, which is a byproduct of the brewing industry, nutritional yeast is primary grown yeast which has been deactivated. It has a strong flavor that adds umami to food. It comes in flakes or powder and can be found in the bulk section of many natural foods stores. I prefer the flakes.

Psyllium Husks: A source of dietary fiber from the husks of a seed. Psyllium is often used as a natural laxative or colon cleansing agent. Psyllium also works well as a thickener or gelling agent, as it can absorb many times its volume of water.

"Raw" Cashews: The shells of cashews contain a caustic toxin; therefore the shells are removed before the cashews are sold to consumers. In most cases, heat is used in the removal of the shells, therefore most cashews are not truly raw. The recipes in this book call for "raw" cashews: those that are sold with the label raw, but that would be more accurately labeled "untoasted" and "unsalted."

Sea Palm Fronds: A sea vegetable that has long leaves with parallel grooves along them. Some sea palm fronds will become tender after a long soak, but some will not become tender without cooking. They are delicious!

Tahini: A spreadable paste made from ground sesame seeds. The recipes in this book use raw tahini, which can be harder to find than roasted but has a more delicate flavor and is healthier.

Tamari: A type of soy sauce that is made with less wheat than regular soy sauce or entirely without wheat. A different process is also used to produce tamari. It has a mellower, richer flavor than regular soy sauce, and is a little less salty. I use gluten-free tamari.

Tempeh: A food made by inoculating soybeans, or soybean and grain mixtures, or other beans and/or grains with mold spores and leaving it in a warm place to culture. Tempeh originated in Indonesia and is quite delicious!

Umeboshi Paste (AKA "ume paste"): Mashed umeboshi plums.

Umeboshi Plums (AKA "ume plums"): A plum-like fruit grown in Japan, fermented in a salt brine with shiso (perilla) leaves. Umeboshi adds a bright, tart, salty flavor to foods.

Umeboshi Vinegar (AKA "ume plum vinegar," "ume vinegar"): Not really vinegar, ume vinegar is actually the brine from the process of fermenting umeboshi plums.

Wakame: A wide-leaved, ruffled sea vegetable, wakame should be soaked for 20 minutes or so before cooking. I like to cut the center rib out after soaking and cook the rib longer than the leaves so both will get tender and delicious. Wakame flakes, AKA "instant wakame," have been precooked and dehydrated. They soak up very quickly for salads or miso soup, growing to many times their size.

Resources to Support Plant Eating

Even though the dominant human dietary pattern in the U.S. and much of the world is omnivorous and to make an alternative choice is countercultural, a rich and plentiful assortment of resources exists to support your journey to a plant-based or plant-rich diet. The short lists of resources in this chapter are meant to be starting points. No doubt you will find your own favorites, and I hope you will share them with me!

ORGANIZATIONS

There are hundreds of wonderful organizations that provide resources to support your transition to a healthier, more environmentally sustainable, more just, and more compassionate diet. Following are a few of my favorites, with excerpted descriptions from their websites and some of the resources they can offer you.

Physicians Committee for Responsible Medicine (pcrm.org). "The Physicians Committee is leading a revolution in medicine—putting a new focus on health and compassion. The Physicians Committee combines the clout and expertise of more than 12,000 physicians with the dedicated actions of 150,000 members across the United States and around the world." PCRM is one of my favorite organizations and the recipient of a portion of the revenue from my book series. The organization is incredibly effective in its work to research, educate, advocate, and create powerful system changes that improve human health, reduce animal suffering, and make the world a better place. A few of the practical resources they offer are the 21-Day Vegan Kickstart program, weekly recipes, trainings for medical professionals, nutrition consultation and health care at their Barnard Medical Center, and information on a variety of nutrition and ethical research topics.

Vegan Outreach (veganoutreach.org). "Vegan Outreach is a…nonprofit organization working to end violence towards animals. Vegan Outreach seeks a future when sentient animals are no longer exploited as commodities." Vegan Outreach distributes millions of high-quality brochures on college campuses, concerts, and festivals, encouraging people to adopt a plant-based diet. In addition to these brochures, other resources include a supportive social media presence, a mentoring program, practical tips, and recipes.

NutritionFacts.org (nutritionfacts.org). "NutritionFacts.org is a strictly non-commercial, science-based public service provided by Dr. Michael Greger, providing free updates on the latest in nutrition research via bite-sized videos." Dr. Greger reads every nutrition journal, then creates interesting and sometimes even funny videos, breaking the science down into language and graphics that are accessible to the layperson. The videos are a great resource for learning about any aspect of nutrition and health and are searchable by topic. I regularly go to nutritionfacts.org to learn what science tells us about nutrition. Regardless of what I hear or see presented in the videos, I trust that Dr. Greger has done sound research, analysis, and reporting, untainted by commercial interests.

A Well-Fed World (awfw.org). "A Well-Fed World is a hunger relief and animal protection organization chipping away at two of the world's most immense, unnecessary and unconscionable forms of suffering… the suffering of people hungry from lack of food, and the suffering of animals used and abused for food." Resources provided by A Well-Fed World include small grants for projects that fit within the scope of their work, and a humane gift-giving program that provides donors with an opportunity to feed hungry families without causing harm to animals.

Farm Sanctuary (farmsanctuary.org). The mission of Farm Sanctuary is "to protect farm animals from cruelty, inspire change in the way society views and treats farm animals, and promote compassionate vegan living." Resources they offer include research grants, a home animal adoption and placement program, tours of their three shelters where visitors can connect with rescued farm animals, and high-quality, low-cost literature.

BOOKS

If you like to read, perhaps one of the following books will be of interest to you and supportive of your movement to a plant-based or plant-rich diet. Some are classics and others are very new releases. Within the small but diverse group of books in this list, you will probably be able to find something of interest to you.

The China Study, T. Colin Campbell, Ph.D. This classic book is a well-researched examination of the connection between nutrition and heart disease, diabetes, and cancer. An updated edition will be coming out soon.

How Not to Die, Michael Greger with Gene Stone. Dr. Michael Greger of NutritionFacts.org has written his first book, and it is on the New York Times bestseller list as of this writing. The book is a science-based guide to nutrition for those wanting to prevent or heal from chronic fatal diseases.

Breaking the Food Seduction: The Hidden Reasons Behind Food Cravings— And 7 Steps to End Them Naturally, or any other book by Dr. Neal Barnard. Dr. Barnard is the President of Physicians Committee for Responsible Medicine. He is a prolific writer whose compelling books illuminate health and nutrition topics with great clarity. This book helps you break free from the addictive nature of unhealthy foods.

Food Rules: An Eater's Manual, Michael Pollan. While bestselling author Michael Pollan does not suggest that everyone adopt a vegan diet, his seven-word rule for eating is "Eat food. Not too much. Mostly plants." In this book, Pollan provides 64 commonsense rules for eating that elaborate on these seven words. This book is great for people wanting to reduce animal product consumption and eat healthy, whole foods.

The Food Revolution: How Your Diet Can Help Save Your Life and Our World, John Robbins. This book and Robbins' earlier book, Diet for a New America, a classic, look at the ethical, health, environmental, economic, and even political aspects of our diets. Robbins encourages people to join a food revolution in which we align our food choices with values of compassion and integrity.

MOVIES

Watching educational movies can be an inspiring way to learn about topics related to our food choices. Movies are also a great way to introduce friends and family members to these important topics. Again, I offer just a nibble from the vast menu of possible movie choices. Please note that many movies about veganism, animal rights, animal agriculture, and similar topics can be very hard to watch because they expose the cruelty and violence of animal agriculture.

Cowspiracy: The Sustainability Secret. I wrote about this movie in the chapter entitled "My Story, or What Drove Me to Write This Book." The movie examines the environmental harm caused by animal agriculture and asks why many of the big environmental organizations are not addressing this. Cowspiracy is a documentary; it is highly informative and also funny at times. There is one very violent scene, but otherwise the film is fairly tame.

Earthlings. I believe that any openhearted person who is willing to watch this film will come away profoundly changed. The movie graphically depicts the myriad ways in which animals are exploited for human economic gain. Be sure to watch this with others.

Forks Over Knives. This film examines the relationship between diet and disease. It focuses on the lives and work of two researchers, Dr. T. Colin Campbell and Dr. Caldwell Esselstyn. Both doctors independently discovered that a whole-food, plant-based diet could prevent, and even reverse, such degenerative conditions as type 2 diabetes, heart disease, and some forms of cancer. Forks Over Knives is packed full of fascinating and eye-opening information, presented in an engaging and captivating manner. This is a must-see film that can change and even save your life!

Vegan Everyday Stories. This charming documentary highlights the lives of four very different "everyday" vegans, including an eight-year-old activist and a former cattle rancher. It also includes appearances by some well-known vegans. There are no visually graphic scenes of violence, but there is one intense scene in which a woman describes what she saw and felt when she visited a slaughterhouse.

ONLINE AND OTHER SOURCES OF INGREDIENTS IN RECIPES

The basics of a nourishing, delicious vegan diet are vegetables, fruits, whole grains, and legumes. Nuts and seeds provide additional nutrition and flavor possibilities. I am fairly confident that these basic foods can be found in most areas of the U.S. and other countries around the globe. I am fortunate to live in an area in which less common vegan foods are also easy to find. In sending recipes to test to friends living in other areas, I learned that not everyone has access to things such as sea vegetables, live sauerkraut, and umeboshi. Fortunately, this is a time in which we can access non-local resources to support our needs, regardless of where we live, at least in the developed world. The following list gives a few sources for the less common ingredients in the recipes, as well as sources of additional whole plant foods.

Azure Standard (azurestandard.com). This large natural and organic food distributor carries a very wide selection of products, many at lower cost than can be found in local retailers. Azure Standard will deliver your order to one of thousands of drop points around the U.S., including Alaska and Hawaii. You can search to see if there is a drop point near you by going to their interactive map: https://www.azurestandard.com/get-started/find-drop. If your order is over $50 and is delivered to a drop point, you will not be charged for delivery. If it is under $50, there is a small order delivery fee of $5. If you are not near a drop point, Azure Standard will ship your order. Unlike some similar services, you do not need to buy large quantities, but it is more economical to do so.

Other Online Bulk Natural and Online Food Sellers. I have done business with Azure Standard for several years and feel very comfortable recommending that company. I like the fact that I can order any quantity and it is delivered to a drop point near me. There are many other online distributors of natural and organic foods. Some sell food in bulk and others sell only packaged food. I found a number of examples via Google searches. If you are out of the delivery area for these distributors, I suggest you conduct a search and make it specific to your area. I acknowledge that some areas of the world may be very poorly served, if at all; however if you are reading this book, it is likely that you will be able to purchase nutritious vegan food online and have it shipped to you. Here are a few sites I found:

- In Canada: Organic Matters, http://www.omfoods.com. Wide variety of foods including bulk and packaged items, manageable quantities, and good prices.
- Delivers in U.S. and internationally: Manna Harvest, http://www.mannaharvest.net. Manageable quantities, great prices on certain foods (e.g. organic nuts, some beans), selection not comprehensive.
- Delivers in 48 U.S. States (not Alaska or Hawaii): Thrive Market, https://thrivemarket.com. Wide variety of packaged food (I didn't see any bulk), great prices, requires membership with $59.95 annual fees.

Item-Specific Sources. The following online retailers are sources for some of the less common ingredients in the recipes.

- Eden Foods, http://www.edenfoods.com. Recipe ingredients available from Eden foods include a wide variety of sea vegetables (e.g. kombu, wakame flakes, arame, hijiki), ume plum vinegar, umeboshi plums and paste, miso, gluten-free tamari, canned beans with no BPA in the lining.
- Lucky Vitamin, https://www.luckyvitamin.com. One of the online retailers for Artisana raw nut butters, coconut butter, and tahini. They also stock

organic psyllium husks and chia seeds.

· Akin's Natural Foods, http://www.akins.com. This online retailer has organic dried chipotle peppers.

· Mountain Rose Herbs, https://www.mountainroseherbs.com. This retailer sells a wide variety of organic bulk spices for reasonable prices, in quantities as low as one ounce. If you can get small quantities of spices in bulk from a store in your local area, that is ideal. If you can't, however, Mountain Rose Herbs has you covered for spices such as those called for in Indian Spiced Beet and Coconut Salad.

Local Sources for Fresh Produce. A phenomenal source for fresh produce in many areas is food grown and harvested on local farms. There are several ways that this food can get from the farm to your table. For instance, you are probably aware of farmers markets held in your area. At these markets you can get truly fresh produce from your geographic region, if not from your local area. Farm stands are another great possibility. One powerful way to get plenty of veggies to increase the vitality of your family while also contributing to the vitality of local farmers is to invest in consumer supported agriculture (CSA). Many farms offer this option to consumers, allowing you to buy a "share" of the harvest for a set fee. Typically, your share of produce will be delivered or available for pick up throughout the season, and the specific vegetables and fruits in the share will shift with seasonal availability.

Notes

MY STORY, OR WHAT DROVE ME TO WRITE THIS BOOK

1. Steinfeld, Henning, *Livestock's Long Shadow: Environmental Issues and Options,* Rome: Food and Agriculture Organization of the United Nations, 2006, 272.

2. Doug Moss & Roddy Scheer, "Have We Passed the Point of No Return on Climate Change?" *Scientific American,* April 13, 2015, http://www.scientificamerican.com/article/have-we-passed-the-point-of-no-return-on-climate-change/ (accessed September 29, 2016); Eric Holthaus, "The Point of No Return: Climate Change Nightmares Are Already Here," *Rolling Stone,* August 5, 2015, http://www.rollingstone.com/politics/news/the-point-of-no-return-climate-change-nightmares-are-already-here-20150805 (accessed September 29, 2016); Michael Slezak, "World's Carbon Dioxide Concentration Teetering on the Point of No Return," *The Guardian,* May 11, 2016, https://www.theguardian.com/environment/2016/may/11/worlds-carbon-dioxide-concentration-teetering-on-the-point-of-no-return (accessed September 29, 2016) This article quoted atmospheric scientist David Etheridge saying, "Even if we stopped emitting now, we're committed to a lot of warming."; Rachel Dicker, "Safe Carbon Levels in the Atmosphere Are Now a Thing of the Past," *U.S. News and World Report,* Sept. 29, 2016, http://www.usnews.com/news/articles/2016-09-29/atmospheric-carbon-dioxide-levels-pass-400-ppm-tipping-point-maybe-for-good (accessed September 29, 2016).

3. This phrase, "a moment of high resolve," is borrowed from Dr. Howard Thurman. It comes from his well-known essay "The Moments of High Resolve," published in *Meditations of the Heart* (Boston: Beacon Press, 1953).

FIVE URGENT REASONS TO EAT MORE PLANTS

4. National Center for Health Statistics, "Leading Causes of Death," Centers for Disease Control and Prevention, http://www.cdc.gov/nchs/fastats/leading-causes-of-death.htm (accessed September 5, 2016).

5. Caldwell B. Esselstyn Jr., et al, "A Way to Reverse CAD?," *Journal of Family Practice* 63.7 (2014): 356-364, quoted in "Breaking Medical News: Plant-Based Diet Reverses Heart Disease," July 1, 2014, Physicians Committee for Responsible Medicine, http://www.pcrm.org/health/medNews/plant-based-diet-reverses-heart-disease (accessed September 6, 2016).

6. Francesca L. Crowe et al., "Risk of Hospitalization or Death from Ischemic Heart Disease Among British Vegetarians and Nonvegetarians: Results from the EPIC-Oxford Cohort," *The American Journal of Clinical Nutrition,* 97, no. 3 (March 2013): 597-603, http://ajcn. nutrition.org/content/97/3/597.long (accessed September 6, 2016). See also Monica Dinu et al., "Vegetarian, Vegan Diets and Multiple Health Outcomes: a Systematic Review with Meta-Analysis of Observational Studies, *Critical Reviews in Food Science and Nutrition* (February 2016), https://www.researchgate.net/profile/Francesco_Sofi/publication/293329136_Vegetarian_vegan_diets_and_multiple_health_outcomes_a_systematic_review_with_meta-analysis_of_observational_studies/links/56c7474e08ae5488f0d2c8f4.pdf (accessed September 16, 2016).

7. Lillie B. Link et al., "Dietary Patterns and Breast Cancer Risk in the California Teachers Study Cohort," *American Journal of Clinical Nutrition* 98, no. 6 (December 2013), https://www. ncbi.nlm.nih.gov/pmc/articles/PMC3831538/ (accessed September 6, 2016).

8. Yessenia Tantamango-Bartley et al., "Are Strict Vegetarians Protected Against Prostate Cancer?" *American Journal of Clinical Nutrition* 103, no. 1 (January 2016): 153-160, http://ajcn. nutrition.org/content/103/1/153.long (accessed September 6, 2016).

9. Monica Dinu et al., "Vegetarian, Vegan Diets and Multiple Health Outcomes: a Systematic Review with Meta-Analysis of Observational Studies," *Critical Reviews in Food Science and Nutrition* (February 2016), https://www.researchgate.net/profile/Francesco_Sofi/publication/293329136_Vegetarian_vegan_diets_and_multiple_health_outcomes_a_systematic_review_with_meta-analysis_of_observational_studies/links/56c7474e08ae5488f0d2c8f4. pdf (accessed September 16, 2016).

10. Yessenia Tantamango-Bartley et al., "Vegetarian Diets and the Incidence of Cancer in a Low-risk Population," *Cancer Epidemiology Biomarkers and Prevention* 22, no. 2 (February 2013): 286-294, http://cebp.aacrjournals.org/content/22/2/286 (accessed September 16, 2016).

11. Stephen JD O'Keefe et al., "Fat, Fibre and Cancer Risk in African Americans and Rural Africans." *Nature Communications* 6 (2015), http://www.nature.com/articles/ncomms7342 (accessed September 16, 2016).

12. Beibei Zhu et al., "Dietary Legume Consumption Reduces Risk of Colorectal Cancer: Evidence from a Meta-Analysis of Cohort Studies." *Scientific Reports* 5 (2015), http://www. nature.com/articles/srep08797?WT.ec_id=SREP-20150310 (accessed September 16, 2016).

13. A group of researchers examined the correlation between diet and Type 2 diabetes using data gathered in three large cohort studies totaling over 200,000 people. Eating a high-quality, plant-based diet was found to substantially reduce the risk for Type 2 diabetes. Ambika Satija et al., "Plant-based Dietary Patterns and Incidence of Type 2 Diabetes in US Men and Women: Results from Three Prospective Cohort Studies," *PLoS Med* 13, no. 6 (2016): e1002039, http://journals.plos.org/plosmedicine/article?id=10.1371/journal. pmed.1002039: e1002039 (accessed September 5, 2016); Campbell S. Rinaldi et al., "A Comprehensive Review of the Literature Supporting Recommendations from the Canadian Diabetes Association for the Use of a Plant-Based Diet for Management of Type 2 Diabetes," *Canadian Journal of Diabetes* (2016), http://www.sciencedirect.com/science/article/ pii/S1499267115300186 (accessed September 5, 2016).

14. For example, the correlation between vegan diets and low levels of obesity has been well established in studies. Nico S. Rizzo et al., "Nutrient Profiles of Vegetarian and Nonvegetarian Dietary Patterns Continuing Professional Education (CPE) Information," *Journal of the Academy of Nutrition and Dietetics* 113, no. 12 (2013): 1610-1619, https://www.researchgate.net/profile/Karen_Jaceldo-Siegl/publication/256289621_Nutrient_Profiles_of_Vegetarian_and_Nonvegetarian_Dietary_Patterns/links/5613fbe408aed47facedfab9.pdf (accessed September 5, 2016). Vegan diets also help with weight loss: a group of researchers studied weight loss among a population randomly assigned to one of five dietary groups. The group consuming a vegan diet demonstrated the highest weight loss and also had improved levels of macronutrients: Gabrielle M. Turner-McGrievy et al., "Comparative Effectiveness of Plant-Based Diets for Weight Loss: a Randomized Controlled Trial of Five Different Diets," *Nutrition* 31, no. 2 (February 2015): 350–358, http://www.nutritionjrnl.com/article/S0899-9007(14)00423-7/abstract (accessed September 5, 2016).

15. Francesca De Filippis et al., "High-level Adherence to a Mediterranean Diet Beneficially Impacts the Gut Microbiota and Associated Metabolome," *Gut* (2015): gutjnl-2015, https://www.researchgate.net/profile/Diana_Serrazanetti/publication/282343967_High-level_adherence_to_a_Mediterranean_diet_beneficially_impacts_the_gut_microbiota_and_associated_metabolome/links/560fe89e08ae483375180d1d.pdf (accessed September 16, 2016).

16. Dean Ornish et al., "Effect of Comprehensive Lifestyle Changes on Telomerase Activity and Telomere Length in Men with Biopsy-Proven Low-Risk Prostate Cancer: 5-Year Follow-up of a Descriptive Pilot Study." *The Lancet Oncology* 14, no. 11 (2013): 1112-1120, http://www.sciencedirect.com/science/article/pii/S1470204513703668 (accessed September 16, 2016).

17. Zhaoli Dai et al., "Adherence to a Vegetable-Fruit-Soy Dietary Pattern or the Alternative Healthy Eating Index is Associated with Lower Hip Fracture Risk among Singapore Chinese." *The Journal of Nutrition* 144, no. 4 (2014): 511-518., https://www.ncbi.nlm.nih.gov/pmc/articles/PMC3952624/ (accessed September 16, 2016).

18. Bonnie A. White et al., "Many Apples a Day Keep the Blues Away–Daily Experiences of Negative and Positive Affect and Food Consumption in Young Adults," *British Journal of Health Psychology* 18, no. 4 (2013): 782-798, http://onlinelibrary.wiley.com/doi/10.1111/bjhp.12021/full (accessed September 16, 2016).

19. Bamini Gopinath et al., "Association Between Carbohydrate Nutrition and Successful Aging Over 10 Years." *The Journals of Gerontology Series A: Biological Sciences and Medical Sciences* (2016): glw091, http://biomedgerontology.oxfordjournals.org/content/early/2016/05/23/gerona.glw091.full (accessed September 16, 2016).

20. Andrew Smyth et al., "Healthy Eating and Reduced Risk of Cognitive Decline a Cohort From 40 Countries," *Neurology* 84, no. 22 (2015): 2258-2265, https://www.ncbi.nlm.nih.gov/pmc/articles/PMC4456656/ (accessed September 16, 2016).

21. William B. Grant, "Using Multicountry Ecological and Observational Studies to Determine Dietary Risk Factors for Alzheimer's Disease," *Journal of the American College of Nutrition* 35, no. 5 (2016): 476-489, http://www.tandfonline.com/doi/abs/10.1080/07315724.2016.1161566 (accessed September 16, 2016).

22. Martha Clare Morris, et al., "Relations to Cognitive Change with Age of Micronutrients Found in Green Leafy Vegetables," *The FASEB Journal* 29, no. 1 Supplement (2015): 260-3, http://www.fasebj.org/content/29/1_Supplement/260.3.short (accessed September 16, 2016).

23. CDC Division of Nutrition, Physical Activity, and Obesity, National Center for Chronic Disease Prevention and Health Promotion, "Prevalence of Childhood Obesity in the United States, 2011-2012," Centers for Disease Control and Prevention, https://www.cdc.gov/obesity/data/childhood.html (accessed September 16, 2016).

24. American Diabetes Association, "Type 2 Diabetes in Children and Adolescents," *Diabetes Care* 23, no. 3 (March 2000): 381-9, http://care.diabetesjournals.org/content/diacare/23/3/381.full.pdf (accessed September 16, 2016).

25. Edwin Rodriguez-Cruz, MD, "Pediatric Hypertension," Medscape, http://emedicine.medscape.com/article/889877-overview#a5 (accessed September 16, 2016).

26. Christopher Matthews, "FAO Newsroom: Livestock a Major Threat to Environment," Food and Agriculture Organization of the United Nations, http://www.fao.org/newsroom/en/News/2006/1000448/index.html (accessed September 18, 2016).

27. Christopher Matthews, "FAO Newsroom: Livestock a Major Threat to Environment," Food and Agriculture Organization of the United Nations, http://www.fao.org/newsroom/en/News/2006/1000448/index.html (accessed September 18, 2016).

28. Beef Research, "How Much Feed and Water are Used to Make a Pound of Beef?" Beef Cattle Research Council, http://www.beefresearch.ca/blog/cattle-feed-water-use/ (accessed September 18, 2016).

29. For instance an article in USA Today says "It takes about 15 pounds of feed to make 1 pound of beef, 6 pounds of feed for 1 pound of pork and 5 pounds of feed for 1 pound of chicken, the Department of Agriculture estimates." I was unable to find the original source of the data, but other writers also provide similar figures. Elizabeth Welse, "Eating can be Energy-Efficient, too," USA Today, http://usatoday30.usatoday.com/news/nation/environment/2009-04-21-carbon-diet_N.htm (accessed September 16, 2016). The following report distinguishes between "live weight" and "edible weight" in arriving at conversion figures of 10:1 and 25:1 respectively: College of Agriculture, Food, and Environment, "Kentucky Poultry Energy Efficiency Project," University of Kentucky, http://www2.ca.uky.edu/poultryprofitability/Production_manual/Chapter2_Broiler_production_facts_and_figures/Chapter2_chicken_consumption.html (accessed September 16, 2016). The highest figures I found in my research were in a report from UNESCO-IHE: M.M. Mekonnen and A.Y. Hoekstra, "The Green, Blue and Grey Water Footprint of Farm Animals and Animal Products," Value of Water Research Report Series no. 48, UNESCO-IHE, Delft, the Netherlands, http://waterfootprint.org/media/downloads/Report-48-WaterFootprint-Animal-Products-Vol2.pdf, accessed September 18, 2016). This report indicated that the average conversion ratio of feed to output worldwide is 47:1 for beef, 4.2:1 for chicken, 5.8:1 for pork, and 30.2:1 for sheep or goats.

30. Proportions of dried corn to cooked hominy from Gourmet Sleuth, "Hominy," Gourmet

Sleuth: The Gourmet Food and Cooking Resource, http://www.gourmetsleuth.com/ingre-dients/detail/hominy (accessed September 19,2016).

31. Tortilla yield from Vespa Woolf, "How to Make Homemade Corn Tortillas With Dried Corn," Delishably, March 16, 2016, https://delishably.com/special-diets/Best-Home-made-Corn-Tortillas (accessed September 19, 2016).

32. Mark Fischetti, "Which Nations Consume the Most Water?," *Scientific American*, June 1, 2012, http://www.scientificamerican.com/article/water-in-water-out/ (accessed September 18, 2016).

33. See, for example: Jo Craven McGinty, "The Numbers Behind Agricultural Water Use,"The Wall Street Jounal, June 21, 2015, http://www.wsj.com/articles/the-numbers-behind-agri-cultural-water-use-1434726353 (accessed September 18, 2016); Alex Park and Julie Lurie, "It Takes How Much Water to Grow an Almond?!" *Mother Jones,* February 24, 2014, http://www.motherjones.com/environment/2014/02/wheres-californias-water-going (accessed September 18, 2016); and Emine Saner, "Almond Milk: Quite Good for You – Very Bad for the Planet , *The Guardian,* October 21, 2015, https://www.theguardian.com/lifeand-style/shortcuts/2015/oct/21/almond-milk-quite-good-for-you-very-bad-for-the-planet (accessed September 18, 2016).

34. "All of the inputs" refers to things such as water to grow alfalfa, other hay products, and grains to feed animals; the water the animal consumes; and the water used in slaughter operations.

35. Grace Communications Foundation, "The Water Footprint of Food," Grace Communica-tions Foundation, http://www.gracelinks.org/1361/the-water-footprint-of-food (accessed September 19, 2016).

36. Elizabeth Armour, "Food Network's Healthy Eats: How Many Almonds in a Serving,"Food Network, http://blog.foodnetwork.com/healthyeats/2013/04/21/how-many-almonds-in-a-serving/ (accessed September 18, 2016).

37. For purposes of determining waste, this reported included manure, wastewater, urine, bedding, poultry litter, and animal carcasses, but did not include airborne pollutants and greenhouse gases: United States General Accounting Office: Resources, Community, and Economic Development Division, *Report to the Honorable Tom Harkin, Ranking Minority Member, Committee on Agriculture, Nutrition, and Forestry, United States Senate: Animal Agriculture Waste Management Practices,* Lawrence J. Dyckman, July, 1999, http://www.gao.gov/archive/1999/rc99205.pdf (accessed September 19, 2016).

38. Steinfeld, Henning, *Livestock's Long Shadow: Environmental Issues and Options,* Rome: Food and Agriculture Organization of the United Nations, 2006, 137-144.

39. Steinfeld, Henning, *Livestock's Long Shadow: Environmental Issues and Options,* Rome: Food and Agriculture Organization of the United Nations, 2006, 142-143, 210-215.

40. Scarborough, Peter, et al., "Dietary greenhouse gas emissions of meat-eaters, fish-eaters, veg-etarians and vegans in the UK," *Climatic Change* 125 no. 2 (July 2014) 125: 179, http://link.springer.com/article/10.1007/s10584-014-1169-1, (accessed online September 18, 2016).

41. Weber, Christopher L., and H. Scott Matthews., "Food-Miles and the Relative Climate Impacts of Food Choices in the United States," *Environmental Science & Technology* 42 no. 10 (2008): 3508-3513, http://pubs.acs.org/doi/full/10.1021/es702969f (accessed September 18, 2016).

42. Steinfeld, Henning, *Livestock's Long Shadow: Environmental Issues and Options,* Rome: Food and Agriculture Organization of the United Nations, 2006, xxi.

43. Robert Goodland and Jeff Anhang, "Livestock and Climate Change: What if the Key Actors in Climate Change are...Cows, Pigs, and Chickens?" *World Watch* 22, no. 6, November/December 2009, 14, http://www.worldwatch.org/files/pdf/Livestock%20and%20Climate%20Change.pdf (accessed September 19, 2016).

44. Robert Goodland and Jeff Anhang, "Livestock and Climate Change: What if the Key Actors in Climate Change are...Cows, Pigs, and Chickens?" *World Watch* 22, no. 6, November/December 2009, 11, http://www.worldwatch.org/files/pdf/Livestock%20and%20Climate%20Change.pdf (accessed September 19, 2016).

45. Different GWP (global warming potentials, expressed as a multiplier compared to CO2) are offered by different sources. The 72 figure is over a 20-year lifespan according to the Intergovernmental Panel on Climate Change, IPCC Fourth Assessment Report: Climate Change 2007, https://www.ipcc.ch/publications_and_data/ar4/wg1/en/ch2s2-10-2.html (accessed September 18, 2016).

46. United States Environmental Protection Agency, Office of Transportation and Air Quality, *Greenhouse Gas Emissions from a Typical Passenger Vehicle* (May 2014), EPA-420-F-14-040a, 2, https://www.epa.gov/sites/production/files/2016-02/documents/420f14040a.pdf (accessed September 19, 2016).

47. United States Environmental Protection Agency, *Development of an Emissions Model to Estimate Methane from Enteric Fermentation in Cattle,* Joseph Mangino, Katrin Peterson, and Hannah Jacobs, https://www3.epa.gov/ttnchie1/conference/ei12/green/mangino.pdf (accessed September 19, 2016).

48. Admittedly, this example is oversimplified. In addition to carbon dioxide, other greenhouse gases released by the car are methane, nitrous oxide, and if the air conditioning system is leaking, hydroflourocarbon. However the EPA says that carbon dioxide comprises 95–99% of the greenhouse gas emissions from a car, after accounting for the various greenhouse warming potential: United States Environmental Protection Agency, Office of Transportation and Air Quality, *Greenhouse Gas Emissions from a Typical Passenger Vehicle* (May 2014), EPA-420-F-14-040a, 3, https://www.epa.gov/sites/production/files/2016-02/documents/420f14040a.pdf, (accessed September 19, 2016). The cow example is also only a partial rendering of the true picture of greenhouse gas emissions, as additional greenhouse gases are also associated with raising cattle. A complete comparison would most likely demonstrate an even greater discrepancy between the global warming potential of one cow versus one car over the course of a year.

49. Steinfeld, Henning, *Livestock's Long Shadow: Environmental Issues and Options,* Rome: Food and Agriculture Organization of the United Nations, 2006, 271.

50. John-Michael Cross and Rachel Pierson, *Short-Lived Climate Pollutants: Why Are They Important?* (Washington, D.C.: Environmental and Energy Study Institute, 2013), http://www.eesi.org/files/FactSheet_SLCP_020113.pdf (accessed September 19, 2016).

51. Gerard Wedderburn-Bisshop and Lefkothea Pavlidis, *Livestock Production And Shorter-Lived Climate Forcers* (London: World Preservation Foundation, 2011), 4.

52. "Addressing Climate Change in the Near Term: Short-Lived Climate Pollutants," Center for Climate and Energy Solutions, http://www.c2es.org/science-impacts/short-lived-climate-pollutants (accessed September 19, 2016); Duncan Clark, "Environment: How long do greenhouse gases stay in the air?" *The Guardian,* https://www.theguardian.com/environment/2012/jan/16/greenhouse-gases-remain-air (accessed September 19, 2016).

53. See, for example, Anthony J. McMichael et al., Food, Livestock Production, Energy, Climate Change, And Health," *The Lancet* 370, no. 9594 (2007): 1253-1263, http://www.cyprus-institute.us/PDF/McMichael-2007-food.pdf (accessed September 19, 2016); Report prepared for the United Kingdom's Committee on Climate Change, *Food, Land and Greenhouse Gases: The Effect of Changes in UK Food Consumption on Land Requirements and Greenhouse Gas Emissions,* Eric Audsley et al., April, 2011, https://dspace.lib.cranfield.ac.uk/bitstream/1826/6496/1/CCC_Food_land_and_GHG_Sep%202011.pdf (accessed September 19, 2016); Elke Stehfest et al., "Climate Benefits of Changing Diet," *Climatic Change* 95, no. 1-2 (2009): 83-102, http://dels.nas.edu/resources/static-assets/banr/AnimalProductionMaterials/StehfestClimate.pdf (accessed September 19, 2016).

54. Food and Agriculture Organization of the United Nations, International Fund for Agricultural Development, and World Food Programme, *The State of Food Insecurity in the World 2015, Meeting the 2015 International Hunger Targets: Taking Stock of Uneven Progress* (Rome, 2015), non-paginated front matter, http://www.fao.org/3/a4ef2d16-70a7-460a-a9ac-2a65a533269a/i4646e.pdf (accessed September 19, 2016).

55. Dr. Richard Oppenlander, "Blog, The World Hunger-Food Choice Connection: A Summary," Comfortably Unaware, April 22, 2012, http://comfortablyunaware.com/blog/the-world-hunger-food-choice-connection-a-summary/ (accessed September 19, 2016).

56. Steinfeld, Henning, *Livestock's Long Shadow: Environmental Issues and Options,* Rome: Food and Agriculture Organization of the United Nations, 2006, 6.

57. Marco H. Springmann et al., "Analysis and Valuation of the Health and Climate Change Cobenefits of Dietary Change," *Proceedings of the National Academy of Sciences* 113, no. 15 (2016): 4146-4151, http://www.pnas.org/content/113/15/4146.full (accessed September 20, 2016).

PLANT-CONSUMPTION FEARS, MYTHS, AND BARRIERS

58. The Healthline Editorial Team, "Kwashiorkor," Healthline, December 21, 2015, http://www.healthline.com/health/kwashiorkor#Overview1 (accessed September 19, 2016).

59. For example: Lillie B. Link et al., "Dietary Patterns and Breast Cancer Risk in the Califor-

nia Teachers Study Cohort," *American Journal of Clinical Nutrition* 98, no. 6 (December 2013), https://www.ncbi.nlm.nih.gov/pmc/articles/PMC3831538/ (accessed September 6, 2016).; Yessenia Tantamango-Bartley et al., "Are Strict Vegetarians Protected Against Prostate Cancer?" *American Journal of Clinical Nutrition* 103, no. 1 (January 2016): 153-160, http://ajcn.nutrition.org/content/103/1/153.long (accessed September 6, 2016); Monica Dinu et al., "Vegetarian, Vegan Diets and Multiple Health Outcomes: a Systematic Review with Meta-Analysis of Observational Studies, *Critical Reviews in Food Science and Nutrition* (February 2016), https://www.researchgate.net/profile/Francesco_Sofi/publication/293329136_Vegetarian_vegan_diets_and_multiple_health_outcomes_a_systematic_review_with_meta-analysis_of_observational_studies/links/56c7474e08ae5488f-0d2c8f4.pdf (accessed September 16, 2016); Stephen JD O'Keefe et al., "Fat, Fibre and Cancer Risk in African Americans and Rural Africans," *Nature Communications* 6 (2015), http://www.nature.com/articles/ncomms7342 (accessed September 16, 2016); Beibei Zhu et al., "Dietary Legume Consumption Reduces Risk of Colorectal Cancer: Evidence from a Meta-Analysis of Cohort Studies," *Scientific Reports* 5 (2015), http://www.nature.com/articles/srep08797?WT.ec_id=SREP-20150310 (accessed September 16, 2016); Ambika Satija et al., "Plant-based Dietary Patterns and Incidence of Type 2 Diabetes in US Men and Women: Results from Three Prospective Cohort Studies," *PLoS Med* 13, no. 6 (2016): e1002039, http://journals.plos.org/plosmedicine/article?id=10.1371/journal.pmed.1002039: e1002039 (accessed September 5, 2016); Campbell S. Rinaldi et al., "A Comprehensive Review of the Literature Supporting Recommendations from the Canadian Diabetes Association for the Use of a Plant-Based Diet for Management of Type 2 Diabetes," *Canadian Journal of Diabetes* (2016), http://www.sciencedirect.com/science/article/pii/S1499267115300186 (accessed September 5, 2016); Nico S. Rizzo et al., "Nutrient Profiles of Vegetarian and Nonvegetarian Dietary Patterns Continuing Professional Education (CPE) Information," *Journal of the Academy of Nutrition and Dietetics* 113, no. 12 (2013): 1610-1619, https://www.researchgate.net/profile/Karen_Jaceldo-Siegl/publication/256289621_Nutrient_Profiles_of_Vegetarian_and_Nonvegetarian_Dietary_Patterns/links/5613fbe408aed47faced-fab9.pdf (accessed September 5, 2016); Gabrielle M. Turner-McGrievy et al., "Comparative Effectiveness of Plant-Based Diets for Weight Loss: a Randomized Controlled Trial of Five Different Diets," *Nutrition* 31, no. 2 (February 2015): 350–358, http://www.nutritionjrnl.com/article/S0899-9007(14)00423-7/abstract (accessed September 5, 2016).

SIX GUIDING PRINCIPLES FOR FABULOUS FLAVOR

60. One of my editors pointed out that the phrase "we are always at choice" is not standard English. This phrase is a statement of principle that would most likely be familiar, however, to people who study New Thought metaphysics or similar philosophies, and to those who have been exposed to popular culture figures who have been influenced by these movements. After my editor made this observation, I did consider changing it to something like "we always have a choice." For me, however, there is more power in the original phrasing. It has an immediacy that is lacking for me in the standard English version. The phrase "we are always at choice" conjures up a mental image of this now moment, this point in time, this place where I am in consciousness right now. In this place, I am always at a point of choice. Acknowledging that I "have" a choice, does not call me up to the same level of accountability as knowing that I am making a choice in this moment, and in this moment,

and in this moment, and that each of these choice points is a place of tremendous potential power. What will you do with the power of your choice of this now moment?

61. See, for example, Kenneth F. Ferraro and Cynthia M. Albrecht-Jensen, "Does Religion Influence Adult Health?" *Journal for the Scientific Study of Religion* 30, no. 2 (1991): 193-202, http://www.jstor.org/stable/1387213?seq=1#page_scan_tab_contents (accessed September 16, 2016.); or Richard Shiffman, "The Blog: Why People Who Pray Are Healthier Than Those Who Don't," Huffington Post, January 18, 2012, http://www.huffingtonpost.com/richard-schiffman/why-people-who-pray-are-heathier_b_1197313.html (accessed September 16, 2016).

62. Robert M. Nerem, Murina J. Levesque, and J. Fredrick Cornhill, "Social Environment as a Factor in Diet-induced Atherosclerosis," *Science* 208, no. 4451 (1980): 1475-1476, cited in "Study Shows Cuddling of Bunnies Helps Keep Their Arteries Clear," *Ocala Star-Banner,* April 13, 1980, https://news.google.com/newspapers?nid=1356&-dat=19800413&id=H35RAAAAIBAJ&sjid=EAYEAAAAIBAJ&pg=7118,4826469&hl=en (accessed September 16, 2016).

RESOURCES TO SUPPORT PLANT EATING

63. "About Us," Physicians Committee for Responsible Medicine, http://www.pcrm.org/about/about/about-pcrm (accessed September 28, 2016).

64. "Mission," Vegan Outreach, http://veganoutreach.org/mission/ (accessed September 28, 2016).

65. "About NutritionFacts.org," NutritionFacts.org, http://nutritionfacts.org/about (accessed September 28, 2016).

66. "Our Mission," A Well-Fed World, http://awfw.org/mission/ (accessed September 28, 2016).

67. "About Us," Farm Sanctuary, http://www.farmsanctuary.org/about-us/ (accessed September 28, 2016).

68. Michael Pollan, *In Defense of Food: The Myth of Nutrition and the Pleasures of Eating* (New York: Penguin Books, 2008), 1.

Keep in Touch

I'D LOVE TO HEAR FROM YOU!

Did you enjoy Sensational Salads to Cool the Earth?
I would love to hear your thoughts about the book and
your suggestions for future books in the Tastes Like Love
series. Contact me at beth@tasteslikelove.com.

I HAVE A GIFT FOR YOU

If you would like a free booklet of
recipes and to stay in the loop about
future book releases, sign up at:

http://tasteslikelove.com/books/gift/

I will send you a PDF booklet via
email. It will contain sample recipes
from at least four of the books in the
Tastes Like Love series.

CPSIA information can be obtained at www.ICGtesting.com
Printed in the USA
LVIW01n2148070617
536948LV00001B/1